Sydney mini

The Essential **Visitors'** Guide

Sydney mini Explorer
ISBN 13 – 978-976-8182-91-3
ISBN 10 – 976-8182-91-1

Copyright © Explorer Group Ltd 2007
All rights reserved.

All maps © Explorer Group Ltd 2007

Front cover photograph – Pete Maloney

Printed and bound by
Emirates Printing Press, Dubai, UAE

Explorer Publishing & Distribution
PO Box 34275, Zomorrodah Building,
Za'abeel Rd, Dubai , United Arab Emirates
Phone (+971 4) 335 3520 **Fax** (+971 4) 335 3529
Email info@explorerpublishing.com
Web www.explorerpublishing.com

While every effort and care has been made to ensure the accuracy of the information contained in this publication, the publisher cannot accept responsibility for any errors or omissions it may contain.

No part of this publication may be reproduced, stored in a retrieval system, or transmitted, in any form or by any means, electronic, mechanical, photocopying, recording or otherwise, without the prior permission in writing of the publisher.

Introduction

Welcome to the *Sydney Mini Explorer*. This book has been lovingly crafted by the same team that brought you *Sydney Explorer: The Complete Residents' Guide*. Written entirely by Sydney locals, we've managed to cram everything from the best pubs to the finest artworks into this mini marvel. If we've missed anything, you want to know more about what we do or you just want to tell us that we're great, please have a look at our website, www.explorerpublishing.com.

The Explorer Team

Contents

2 **Essentials**
- 4 G'day
- 6 Sydney Checklist
- 16 Best of Sydney
- 18 Visiting Sydney
- 22 Local Knowledge
- 28 Media & Further Information
- 30 Public Holidays & Annual Events
- 36 Getting Around
- 42 Places to Stay

50 **Exploring**
- 52 Explore Sydney
- 54 At a Glance
- 56 Bondi & Around
- 62 CBD
- 68 Circular Quay & The Rocks
- 74 Darling Harbour & Chinatown
- 80 The Harbour
- 84 Manly
- 90 North Sydney
- 94 Further Out
- 100 Tours & Sightseeing

108 **Sports & Spas**
- 110 Activities
- 118 Spectator Sports
- 122 Spas & Massage Centres

Sydney mini Explorer

128 Shopping
- 130 Shopping Sydney
- 132 Hotspots
- 136 Markets
- 138 Shopping Malls
- 142 Department Stores
- 144 Where To Go For…

150 Going Out
- 152 Restaurants by Cuisine
- 154 Social Sydney
- 158 Bondi
- 162 CBD
- 170 Circular Quay & The Rocks
- 174 Darling Harbour & Chinatown
- 178 Kings Cross & Woolloomooloo
- 184 Manly
- 188 Newtown
- 192 North Sydney
- 194 Surry Hills & Darlinghurst
- 200 Entertainment

204 Profile
- 206 Culture
- 210 History
- 218 Sydney Today

222 Maps

246 Index

Essentials

- **4** G'day
- **6** Sydney Checklist
- **16** Best of Sydney
- **18** Visiting Sydney
- **22** Local Knowledge
- **28** Media & Further Information
- **30** Public Holidays & Annual Events
- **36** Getting Around
- **42** Places to Stay

Essentials

Essentials

G'day

Welcome to pretty beaches and rugged cliffs, the sparkling harbour with its iconic bridge and the graceful sails of the Opera House. Welcome to Sydney.

This buzzing, cosmopolitan city is admired for its natural attractions and envied for its incredible, outdoorsy lifestyle. Beneath the splendid surface of its harbour and beaches you'll discover a vibrant cafe culture, historic pubs, fantastic seafood and a wild nightlife. Its short but colourful history is everywhere – in the solid sandstone alleyways of The Rocks, at the Aboriginal rock carvings near Bondi and Manly, and among the eclectic architectural mix of high-rise office blocks and stately Victorian buildings.

Sydney's attraction lies in its mix of city life and a gorgeous natural environment. With a magnificent harbour as its focus, sandstone cliffs, pretty bays, long stretches of beach and brilliant natural light, Sydney's untainted setting rivals any other city in the world.

Sydney is a young, vibrant place that throws together innumerable groups and cultures. From corporate climbers and degenerate boozers to sports nuts, surfers and artists, the whole world is here.

Its iconic images may make you feel as though you've been here before, but there is more to this city than the Opera House and the Harbour Bridge. This book aims to help you find out what's what.

The bridge and Opera House at dusk

This chapter, Essentials, has all the bits for planning your trip. We've tried to cover anything you may need to know in advance, like possible itineraries, visas and money, how to get about and where to stay. We've also suggested some 'must-dos', which begin on the next page.

In Exploring, we've carved the city up into its main areas and highlighted the best bits, like museums and beaches. Sports & Spas highlights the many chances to get active here, watch a big game, or be shamelessly pampered. Going Out again divides the city, but this time with eating, drinking and other entertainment in mind. Because, Sydney has become Australia's foodie capital, and with all the exotic eateries crammed into its suburban streets, you'll need some guidance about where to begin. The Profile chapter offers a little bit of backstory, covering Sydney's short but colourful past. And Shopping is all about shopping, but you probably worked that out for yourself.

Essentials

G'day

Essentials

Sydney Checklist

01 Climb the Bridge

It will be among the first questions asked of you by friends back home; 'did you climb the bridge?' This iconic structure is just begging to be conquered. And if heights give you the wobbles, the lookout tower is a decent second best. See p.68.

02 Sail the Harbour

Sydney is a harbour-centric city, and the views from the water are lovely. You can admire the scenery from a luxury catamaran, or get a bit more involved by learning to sail or hiring kayaks and paddling through middle harbour. See p.113.

Essentials

Sydney Checklist

Essentials

Sydney Checklist

03 Surf Bondi

This famous crescent-shaped strip of sand gave birth to the enduring Aussie cliche of sun-loving, surf-mad larrikins. It's also the symbolic home of the iconic Bondi Surf Bathers Life Saving Club with their natty red hats and skimpy little trunks. See p.116

Sydney **mini** Explorer

04 Paddington Markets

This is where residents snaffle local designer fashion, jewellery and homewares at negotiable prices, laze over a coffee or try a tarot reading. There's no tacky Australiana souvenirs in sight and it's smack bang in the middle of Oxford Street. See p.137.

Essentials

Sydney Checklist

05 Taronga Zoo

Beyond the native Australian attractions and the exotic overseas imports (giraffes, penguins and Asian elephants), locals return here for the impressive view across the harbour to the towering city skyline. To find out more, see p.91.

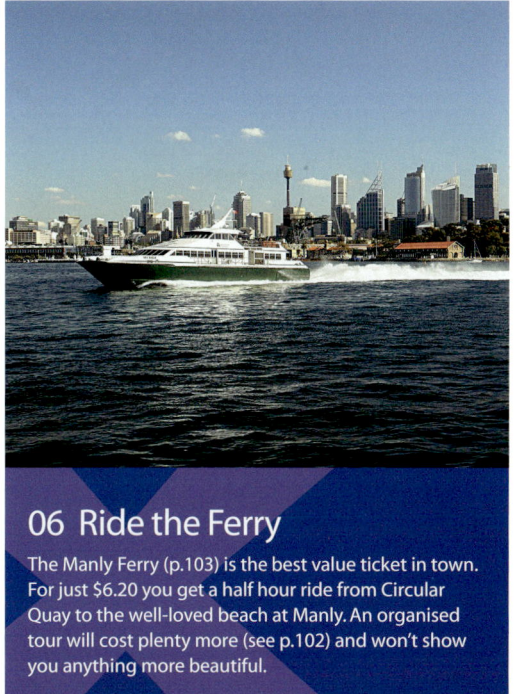

06 Ride the Ferry

The Manly Ferry (p.103) is the best value ticket in town. For just $6.20 you get a half hour ride from Circular Quay to the well-loved beach at Manly. An organised tour will cost plenty more (see p.102) and won't show you anything more beautiful.

Essentials

Sydney Checklist

Essentials

Sydney Checklist

07 Botanic Gardens

Picnic in the Royal Botanic Gardens, where local families and canoodling couples unpack hampers every weekend. Directly on the harbour, this grassy expanse is a gorgeous place to wile away a summer's afternoon and escape the city. See p.65.

08 Catch a Game

This sports mad city has plenty of big events from basketball to Aussie rules. If you're in town at the right time, try a cricket game at the SCG (p.119) or see the brutal, fascinating spectacle that is the Rugby League State of Origin match (p.120).

Essentials

Sydney Checklist

Essentials

Sydney Checklist

09 The Cross

Despite its reputation, it's not all debauchery and drugs in Kings Cross. You'll still stumble across some dodgy characters, but the police presence makes you feel safe, and it's a colourful contrast to the ritzier eastern suburbs. Get amongst it from p.178 onwards.

Essentials

Sydney Checklist

10 Walk the Cliffs

Sydney's weather-beaten coastline has some glorious foot trails. Locals never tire of the path from Bondi to Bronte (p.59) with its spectacular ocean views. Bondi to Coogee and the four-hour Spit Bridge to Manly hike are just as impressive. See p.59 and p.85.

Best of Sydney

Essentials

For Drinkers...

Sydney is a welcoming place for those that like the sauce, what with its 24 hour pubs with in-house ATMs. But there are some swanky spots too, around Circular Quay (p.170) in the CBD (p.162) and over in Bondi (p.158). There are some more cutting edge spots to be found in Kings Cross (p.178) and Darlinghurst (p.194) as well. For those that prefer a little taste of grape, Sydney is just a few hours away from some lovely wineries. Head north to the Hunter Valley (p.94), south to the Southern Highlands (p.98) and drive about, tasting to your tongue's content (with a designated driver of course), or take one of the organised wine tours listed on p.107.

For Art Lovers...

Sydney's impressive natural gifts have proved inspirational to artists for more than 25,000 years. Some Aboriginal rock art can still be found in the sandstone near Terrey Hills. More recently, local artists Arthur Boyd and Brett Whitely have celebrated the city's scenery. The Art Gallery of New South Wales (p.63) and the Museum of Contemporary Art (p.70) are worth half a day each for proper art hounds. The S.H. Ervin gallery (p.70), down in The Rocks, has a salon de refuses that takes in the rejects from the Archibald Prize and can turn up some interesting little gems. The Gavala Aboriginal Art and Cultural Centre (p.74) is the only gallery in the city that is dedicated to indigenous works. The Manly Art Gallery & Museum (p.84) is also worth a look.

Sydney **mini** Explorer

For History Buffs...

Despite is relative youth as a 'western' nation, Australia has a rich and colourful history. To get an idea of the 40,000 years before European settlement, take one of the Aboriginal heritage tours that run from the Royal Botanic Gardens (p.65). Speeding forward a few millennia, the National Maritime Museum (p.75) paints an impressive picture of Australia's nautical history, while the Museum of Sydney (p.64) focusses on the city itself. Manly Quarantine Station (p.86) is an interesting reminder of the harshness of Australia's birth as a colony and The Rocks Walking Tours (p.107) give a good show of the murkier elements of the city's past.

For Water Babies...

There's not much in Australia's middle, and the country's natural predilection for port cities has created a nation of watersports enthusiasts. No visit to Sydney would be complete without having a go at surfing on either Bondi (p.57) or Manly (p.85) beaches. Lessons (p.116) are available for those that want a headstart. Or, for a more leisurely approach, charter a boat (p.113) for a cruise around the magnificent harbour. Scuba fans are also well catered for, with plenty of diving (p.111) options, while at the Sydney Aquarium (p.76) or Oceanworld in Manly (p.86) you can nose about the marine life without getting your feet wet. Alternatively, if you just fancy a bit of a paddle or a few lengths, try one of the city's open air pools (p.117), like Icebergs (p.117) down in Bondi.

Visiting Sydney

While the Aussies tend to be welcoming, they are quite protective of their borders. So, make sure everything is in order before you head Down Under.

Getting There

Sydney Kingsford (SYD) is Australia's air transport hub. It is currently undergoing an extensive revamp, due for completion in 2010, but a curfew on flying after 23:00 means delays can be a problem. Direct flights are available across Australia and to Asia Pacific, the Americas and Europe. Australia's size means interstate trips are often made by plane. Budget airlines like REX (Regional Express), Virgin Blue and Jetstar offer low fare flights across the country.

From the Airport

The Sydney Buses service between Bondi Junction and Burwood includes the T1 international and T3 domestic terminals. Clearly marked bus stops are on the Arrivals level of each of these terminals. Information about fares, timetables and connections to other parts of Sydney is available at www.sydneybuses.info or 13 1500. The KST Sydney Airporter (www.kst.com.au, 02 9666 9988) is one of the many shuttle services that run to and from the airport. A single into the centre of Sydney costs $10 and will stop directly at your hotel or apartment block. The Airport Link rail service (www.airportlink.com.au or 13 1500) runs from international and

Airlines

Aerolineas Argentina	02 9234 9000	www.aerolineas.com.ar
Aeropelican	13 1313	www.aeropelican.com.au
Air Canada	02 9232 5222	www.aircanada.com
Air China	02 9232 7277	www.china-airlines.com
Air France	1300 390 190	www.airfrance.com
Air India	02 9299 1983	www.airindia.com
Air New Zealand	13 2476	www.airnewzealand.com.au
Big Sky Express	1800 008 759	www.bigskyexpress.com.au
British Airways	1300 767 177	www.britishairways.com
Cathay Pacific	13 1747	www.cathaypacific.com
Emirates	1300 303 777	www.emirates.com
Freedom Air	1800 122 000	www.freedomair.com.nz
Garuda Indonesia	1300 365 330	www.garuda-indonesia.com
JAL (Japan Airlines)	02 9272 1111	www.jal.co.jp
Jetstar	13 1538	www.jetstar.com
Lufthansa Airlines	02 9367 3800	www.lufthansa.com
Malaysia Airlines	13 2627	www.malaysiaairlines.com.my
Philippine Airlines	02 9650 2188	www.philippineairlines.com
Qantas	13 1313	www.qantas.com.au
REX (Regional Express)	13 1713	www.regionalexpress.com.au
Royal Brunei Airlines	1300 721 271	www.bruneiair.com
Singapore Airlines	13 1011	www.singaporeair.com
SwissAir	02 9231 3744	www.swiss.com
Thai Airways	1300 651 960	www.thaiair.com
United Airlines	13 1777	www.ual.com
Virgin Atlantic	1300 727 340	www.virgin-atlantic.com
Virgin Blue	13 6789	www.virginblue.com.au

Essentials

Visiting Sydney

domestic terminals to Central station, where you can link up to the CityRail network (see p.40). It goes every ten minutes, taking ten to 13 minutes, from 05:20 to 00:30 in the week and 05:10 to 00:46 at weekends. A taxi ride, from the ranks outside each terminal, will cost $30-$35 down to Citcular Quay.

People with Disabilities

The website www.accessibility.com.au gives detailed information on accessible venues in Sydney. It also has a map of accessible parking spaces in the CBD. Information about transport can be found on the transport infoline (telephone 13 1500, TTY 1800 637 500) or at www.sydneytransport.net. au. Accessible Sydney buses display the wheelchair symbol. All monorail trains are accessible. Taxis can be hailed from the street or at taxi ranks. There is no 'lift' fee. To book a wheelchair accessible taxi, call 02 8332 0200.

Visas

Anyone who is not an Australian citizen needs a valid visa to enter the country. You should get this in advance, as airlines may refuse permission to board otherwise. An Electronic Travel Authority (ETA) also allows travel to Australia for a short stay. The ETA is available online (www.eta.immi.gov.au) and from some travel agencies, airlines and Australian visa offices overseas. It costs $20. The tourist visa (subclass 676) is valid for a stay of three, six or 12 months and costs $70. You can also get these online (website as before) and they are granted for single and multiple entries.

Customs

Australia is extremely strict about quarantine procedures. You must declare all food, plant and animal products on arrival. If you're not sure about an item, ask a quarantine officer or call, for free, on 1800 020 504. Adults can bring in the following: $900 worth of goods including gifts, electronic equipment, and jewellery; 2.25 litres of alcoholic drinks; 250 cigarettes or 250 grams of cigars or tobacco products and one opened packet containing 25 cigarettes or less.

Visitor Information in Sydney

There are a number of tourist information offices dotted about the city and a well stocked booth at the airport. For swotting up in advance, try www.sydneyvisitorcentre.com.

Tourist Information	
Manly Visitor Centre	02 9976 1430
Parramatta Visitor Centre	02 8839 3311
Sydney Harbour National Park	02 9247 5033
Sydney Visitor Centre	02 9240 8788

Embassies & Consulates in Sydney	
Canada	02 9364 3000
Ireland	02 9231 6999
New Zealand	02 8256 2000
South Africa	02 6273 2424
United Kingdom	02 9247 7521
USA	02 9373 9200

Essentials — Local Knowledge

Climate

New South Wales is in the temperate zone so the climate is generally mild, although it can be very hot in the northwest and very cold on the southern tablelands. The western suburbs of Sydney have a reputation for severe storms between November and March. Rainfall is spread throughout the year but it is generally wetter from February to June. Summer daytime temperatures can range from 27ºC at the coast to 38ºC inland. Winter temperatures tend to differ less, although overnight it's colder inland.

Sydneysiders know about the dangers of the sun but visitors often learn the hard way. As the song goes, wear sunscreen. Or even better, sunblock. The Skin Cancer Council of NSW claims one in 24 males and one in 35 females will develop malignant skin cancer by age 75. You may hear Australians refer to 'slip-slop-slap'. This campaign encourages people to slip on a shirt, slop on sunscreen and slap on a hat - especially young children.

Crime & Safety

Sydney is safer than many big cities. However, common sense should still apply. Keep alert when travelling on public transport after dark. Make use of Nightsafe areas on train platforms and choose a carriage near the guard's van (the one with a blue light). It's a good idea to keep photocopies of valuable documents in a separate place. Don't leave bags visible in a parked car. Keep handbags closed and firmly attached to you, and keep any luggage in full view. When out and about, avoid dark and deserted areas.

Dos & Don'ts
Smoking is becoming a no-no in Sydney. In New South Wales, legislation is up for discussion that will ban smoking in cars with children as passengers. Pubs and hotels have to limit the area in which they allow smoking. Drinking and driving is a very big don't, as is speeding.

Electricity & Water
Electrical current is 220/240 volts AC and three-pin or two-pin plugs are used. Tap water is perfectly drinkable, though many prefer the taste of bottled water. Some drought restrictions currently apply.

Lost & Found
Should you lose (or find) property on any public transport service, you can contact the relevant company. Visit www.131500.com.au or call 13 1500.

Emergency Numbers	
American Express	1300 132 639
Dentist	02 9369 7050
MasterCard	1800 120 113
Pharmacy	02 9467 7100
Poisons Information Centre	13 1126
Police/Fire/Ambulance/Coastguard	000
Visa International	1800 450 346

Police

The New South Wales Police is Australia's biggest police organisation, with 15,000 officers and more than 500 stations. It has much more power than state police forces in other federal countries like the US or Canada. All police carry guns. They are easily recognised by the blue and white chequered band on their cars. The uniform is quite paramilitary in style, with navy blue cargo pants and baseball cap, a light blue shirt and a leather jacket for winter. In emergencies dial, 000. Otherwise, use the Police Assistance Line on 13 1444.

Money

The most common methods of payment in Sydney are cash, credit card, debit card and cheque. Foreign currencies are not generally accepted. Banks are generally open from 09:30 to 16:00 Monday to Thursday, and on Friday from 09:30 to 17:00. You'll find ATMs in banks, shopping centres and in some bars and clubs. They normally accept debit cards that operate internationally, such as Cirrus and Maestro. International credit cards such as Mastercard, Visa and American Express are all normally accepted in Australian ATMs for cash withdrawals. Traveller's cheques are not generally accepted beyond big stores and hotels. Major international credit cards are widely accepted in restaurants and shops or when booking tours and the like.

Exchange Centres	
American Express	1300 139 060
Thomas Cook	1800 637 642
Travelex	02 9264 1267

The safest place to see sharks is Sydney Aquarium (p.76)

Spiders, Sharks & Stingers

Australia's notorious arachnids can be found in urban areas. The Sydney funnel-web can be identified by the silk 'trip-lines' from the entrance to their webs. For all spiders, except funnel-webs and mouse spiders, if bitten, simply apply an ice-pack to relieve pain. For suspected funnel-web or mouse spider bites, a pressure bandage should be applied and the victim kept calm and quiet until medical attention can be given. Funnel-webs often fall into swimming pools and can appear to be drowned, but can survive 24-30 hours under water.

In the case of a redback bite, seek immediate medical attention. Redbacks can be found in garden sheds, under steps or logs and around swimming pools or piles of rubbish.

In the last 50 years there have been 61 deaths in Australia as a result of shark attacks. Nine of these were in waters off the coast of NSW. However, the chances of attack are minute.

The blue-lined octopus is common to Sydney. These venomous creatures are very shy and will dart away if they see you. All species are brown and only display brilliant blue markings when they feel threatened. The colour may tempt children to pick them up and there have been several fatalities as a result. Sydney's jellyfish can deliver a nasty sting, but these are rarely fatal. If you do get stung, apply liberal doses of vinegar and seek medical attention.

Telephone & Internet

Public payphones in Sydney accept coins or phone cards. International calls can be dialed directly using the prefix 0011 then the number, including country code (see coverflaps for more useful numbers). The blue payphones are privately managed by small businesses and only accept Australian coins. International calling cards are available in denominations of $5 to $50 at newsagents, kiosks or anywhere that displays the Telstra logo. These cards are the most convenient and cheapest way to phone home. There are internet cafes all over the city. Rates start at $3 per hour.

Wireless access is available at the airport. You can sign up at www.sydneyairport.com.au. Public Networks Australia (PubNet) operates free wireless hotspots. Visit www.public.net.au.

Where's Wireless?

Wireless hotspots can be found at Sydney Airport, The Rocks, some McDonald's restaurants, Starbucks cafes, some hotels, Qantas Club lounges, Gloria Jeans cafes, Metropolitan cafes and some bookstores.

Time
Australian Eastern Standard Time (AEST) is equivalent to UCT (formerly GMT) plus 10 hours. In Daylights Savings Time (October to March) clocks go forward one hour.

Tipping
Tipping is entirely up to you. If the service is good, tip 10% of the total bill. For porters, calculate $2 per bag. It is not the custom to tip bar staff or doormen.

Toilets
Public loos are a rarity in Sydney, and pubs and bars occasionally put up signs discouraging toilet use by non-patrons. Large parks often have a public lavatory and there are a few large grey-green cubicles dotted about the city.

Postal Services
Stamps (available from supermarkets and newsagents) for a letter to Europe or America cost $1.85. Post office hours are 09:00 to 17:00, Monday to Friday. The Australia Post HQ at 1 Martin Place also opens until 14:00 on Saturdays. If you are looking to send larger items, see the table of courier companies.

Courier Companies

Australia Post	13 1318	www.auspost.com.au
DHL	13 1406	www.dhl.com.au
Federal Express	13 2610	www.fedex.com.au
UPS	13 1877	www.ups.com

Media & Further Information

Newspapers & Magazines
Sydney has two dailies; *The Sydney Morning Herald* (*The Sun-Herald* on Sundays) and *The Daily Telegraph*. The former has in-depth domestic and international news coverage, solid business and culture reporting. The latter is more populist, but not necessarily sensationalist. *MX* is given away at CityRail stations. *The Australian* and *The Australian Financial Review* are the only national dailies. You can buy newspapers and magazines (including international press) at newsagents, near stations and in shopping centres.

Television
Australia has five terrestrial English language channels. ABC and SBS are government funded. The former is a showcase for Aussie TV talent, but also buys in a lot of BBC programmes from the UK. SBS shows European football, foreign films and has a multicultural programming remit but suffers from poor funding. Both are good for documentaries, news and current affairs. Seven, Nine and Ten are commercial channels, heavy on the ads and US shows.

Radio
Triple J (105.7FM) is perhaps the best known music channel and tries to push new talent. Triple M (104.9FM) plays solid rock. WSFM (101.7FM) plays classics, Mix (106.5FM) is all unobtrusive pop and SBS (97.7FM) produces multicultural shows. On the AM dial, talk is king and 2UE (954) has some of the city's gobbier chatshows. NewsRadio (630) provides rolling news.

Books & Maps

For a colourful historical guide, take a copy of Ruth Park's *Sydney* and start your own private tour at The Rocks. Geoffrey Moorhouse describes the city with true insight, covering history, culture, and political intrigues in *Sydney, The Story of a City*. *The Fatal Shore*, by Robert Hughes, is the granddaddy of Australian popular history books. *Leviathan: The Unauthorised Biography of Sydney*, by John Birmingham, is an entertaining look at the dark side of the city's past. If you're thinking of living here, the Sydney Residents' Guide, from Explorer, is invaluable. Another good resource is Gregory's *Compact Street Directory*.

Websites

www.kidfriendly.com.au	Children's activities
www.cityofsydney.nsw.gov.au	City information
www.whereis.com.au	Interactive street atlas
www.sydneyeguide.com	Official e-guide
www.yellowpages.com.au	Online phone book
www.sydneypubguide.net	Pub listings by area
www.ticketmaster.com.au	Ticket sales
www.discoversydney.com.au	Tourist information
www.sydneyinformation.com	Tourist information
www.visitnsw.com.au	Tourist information
www.131500.com	Transport infoline
www.bugaustralia.com	Traveling on a budget
www.bom.gov.ae	Weather forecast

Public Holidays & Annual Events

Sydneysiders welcome any excuse for a party. From a gay mardi gras to a grungy music festival, it's all covered here.

National public holidays apply across Australia. There are also public holidays that apply to individual states and territories. For example, every November, a half-day holiday applies to the Muswellbrook Shire Council area for the Musswellbrook Cup Race Carnival. There are 25 of these holidays dotted around NSW through 2007. Where fixed holidays fall on a Sunday, the public holiday carries over to the following Monday. For a complete listing, including local holidays, visit www.industrialrelations.nsw.gov.au/holidays.

Public Holidays

Anzac Day	April 25
Australia Day	January 26
Bank Holiday*	First Monday in August
Boxing Day	December 26
Christmas Day	December 25
Easter Monday	March 24, 2008
Easter Saturday	March 22, 2008
Good Friday	March 21, 2008
Labour Day	First Monday in October
New Year's Day	January 01
Queen's Birthday Holiday	Second Monday in June

*Not a state-wide public holiday

Bondi Beach

Essentials

Public Holidays & Annual Events

Public Holidays & Annual Events

The Sydney Festival
Various locations
January
www.sydneyfestival.org.au

This is a prestigious arts festival held for the month of January each year. The Jazz in The Domain and Symphony in The Domain concerts are held as part of the festival. It includes the Bacardi Latin Festival in Darling Harbour, which involves a week of Latin dancing and music.

Flickerfest
Bondi Pavilion
January
www.flickerfest.com.au

This international short film festival has now been running for 16 years. Films from Australia and around the world are screened over ten days at the Bondi Pavilion. Since 2003, it has been included as a qualifying festival for the Best Short Film and Best Animation categories of the Oscars.

Twilight at Taronga Series
Taronga Zoo
January - March
www.zoo.nsw.gov.au

Three months of regular twilight performances at Taronga Zoo. Music ranges from tribute acts and show tunes to modern jazz.

Australia Day
Various locations
January
www.australiaday.gov.au

A number of events are held in and around the harbour, including a parade of ships and the popular race between Sydney's ferry fleet. There is a fireworks display in Darling Harbour in the evening.

Gay and Lesbian Mardi Gras
Various locations
March
www.mardigras.org.au

This festival, organised by and for the gay community, is one of the world's biggest such events. It lasts for a month and includes sports, cultural and arts events and culminates in the flamboyant Mardi Gras parade in Darlinghurst on the first Saturday of March each year. The festival began as a street protest and has grown into a huge celebration.

Royal Easter Show
Sydney Olympic Park
April
www.eastershow.com.au

This is the biggest agricultural show in New South Wales and the largest annual event staged in Australia. Around one million people go each year. The show runs for 14 days over the Easter period.

Rugby League State of Origin
Telstra Stadium
June
www.rleague.com

This sporting contest between the Queensland Maroons and the New South Wales Blues has been going for decades. Club loyalties are set aside for this three-match series as players turn out for the state in which they first played senior rugby. It is considered to be the highlight of rugby league, draws massive TV audiences and is fiercely competitive.

Tri-Nations Rugby
Telstra Stadium
July
www.rugby.com.au

The six match rugby union series was started in 1996 between Australia, New Zealand and South Africa sees the

Wallabies, All Blacks and Springboks fight it out to the bitter end, each determined to take home the trophy.

Rugby League Grand Final — September
Telstra Stadium — www.nrl.com.au
This is the world's most attended rugby league competition and is considered by many to be the most competitive. It is the climax of the National Rugby League season and is held in Sydney in alternate years.

Manly International Jazz Festival — Sept. - October
Various locations — www.manly.nsw.gov.au
The festival takes place over the NSW Labor Day long weekend. All sorts of jazz tastes are catered for, and many of the events are free. The festival is well established on the international scene and is coming up to its 30th anniversary.

Homebake Festival — December
The Domain — www.homebake.com.au
This is a rock/alternative/dance festival featuring only Australian acts, which has been held annually for over 10 years. Audiences get the chance to see emerging talent.

Bondi Beach Christmas Party — December
Bondi Beach — www.waverley.nsw.gov.au
Travellers get together to celebrate Christmas on the sands rather than in the snow. Entertainment is provided but be aware that alcohol is now a no-no in much of the area, after previous parties got out of hand.

Sydney to Hobart Yacht Race December
Sydney Harbour www.rolexsydneyhobart.com
Australia's premier yacht racing event attracts competitors from all over the world. The start, in Sydney Harbour, is spectacular and popular viewing.

New Year's Eve December
Various locations www.sydneynewyearseve.com.au
Sydney has a world-renowned fireworks display that centres around Sydney Harbour, including fireworks shot from the bridge itself. There is a family show at 21:00 and the major fireworks display at midnight. Hundreds of thousands of people gather at vantage points around the harbour.

Essentials

Getting Around

Sydney's centre is small enough to be investigated on foot, and there are plenty of options for exploring the rest of town.

Ferry

Ferries are an integral part of the Sydney landscape and regular routes are as memorable as the scenic tours on offer. The trips to Manly, Watsons Bay and Taronga Zoo are particularly impressive. Circular Quay is the hub for all ferry services. During peak periods, the Jetcat operates between Circular Quay and Manly. It costs $7.90, compared to $6.20 for a regular single. Ferry services also run up to Parramatta, the trip taking around 50 minutes on the Rivercat. Information is available from kiosks at Circular Quay or through the Sydney Transport infoline. Go to www.131500.com.au or call 13 1500. The Sydney Ferries website is www.sydneyferries.nsw.gov.au. The best, and cheapest, option are the FerryTen tickets. These cover ten single trips, with no expiry date. There are five different types each covering varying distances.

Water Taxi

This is a fun but expensive way to get about the harbour, so it pays to share the journey. A private trip from Circular Quay to Darling Harbour can cost around $75 for up to four passengers. Alternatively, shuttle rates start around $15 for adults and $10 for children. You can also order a private water limousine service, seating up to 17 passengers - visit www.

watertaxis.com.au or call Water Taxis Combined on 9555 8888. Other firms include Yellow Water Taxis (1300 138 840) and Watertaxi (02 9211 7730).

Bus

State Transit Authority buses, called Sydney Buses, cover most of eastern Sydney. Private bus companies cover the south and the west. Routes are numbered according to their area. So, 100s serve the northern beaches, 200s the north shore, 300s the eastern suburbs, 400s the inner west and south to Rockdale and Miranda and the 500s and 600s the west, including Ryde and Parramatta. When a route has an L, E or X in its number, it means it is an express route or has limited stops. Fares range from $1.70 to $5.50. Main city terminuses are at Circular Quay, Wynyard, Town Hall and Central stations. The two main tourist shuttle buses, the Sydney Explorer (great name) and the Bondi Explorer, provide a guidebook and recorded commentary. Visit www.sydneybuses.info to plan your exact trip or call the Transport Info Line on 13 1500. You can buy single fares from the driver (excluding "Prepay Only" bus services)

> **Long Distance Coaches**
> Interstate coaches go from Sydney Coach Terminal (02 9212 3433) at Central station. It's open from 06:00-22:30 and ticket offices can also be found here. The bigger firms include Greyhound (www.greyhound.com.au, 13 2030); Premier (www.premierms.com.au, 13 3410); and Murrays (www.murrays.com.au, 13 2251).

but have the correct change ready. TravelTen tickets allow you to buy ten trips at once with no expiry date. DayTripper tickets include unlimited travel on bus, ferry and train services until 04:00. BusTripper allows unlimited travel on all regular Sydney buses for one day. Adult, $11.30; child, $5.60. A one day combined Sydney and Bondi Explorer ticket costs $39.00 (Child $19). The ticket includes travel on regular Sydney buses eastwards of Circular Quay. The ticket will also get you discount offers at various popular attractions.

Car

Australians drive on the left hand side of the road. You are allowed to drive on a current overseas licence for up to three months after arriving in Australia – keep it with you at all times. If your overseas licence is not in English you need to carry an official translation.

The general speed limit in towns is 60kph but many suburban roads have a 50kph limit. The maximum speed on highways in New South Wales is 100kph and on motorways and freeways it is 110kph. Heavy penalties apply for speeding. When covering long distances, be aware of driver

Car Rental Agencies

Avis	13 6333	www.avis.com.au
Budget	13 2727	www.budget.com.au
Europcar	1300 131 390	www.europcar.com.au
Hertz	1300 132 607	www.hertz.com.au
Thrifty	1300 367 227	www.thrifty.com.au

fatigue. Police conduct regular random breath checks and if you are driving it is better not to drink at all, though the legal alcohol limit for fully licensed drivers is 0.05g/100ml. Everyone must wear seatbelts and children need child restraints or baby capsules. For further information, contact the Roads and Traffic Authority, NSW on 13 2213. Car rental prices are variable but range roughly from $47 per day for a compact manual with air conditioning to $70 per day for a big automatic with air conditioning.

Bicycle

Cycling around the CBD is not for the faint-hearted, but the Roads and Traffic Authority NSW has a network of routes around Sydney. Visit www.rta.nsw.gov.au for maps of these and other information for cyclists. *Cycling Around Sydney*, by Bruce Ashley, gives details on longer rides. Visit the publishers at www.bicyclensw.org.au.

Taxi

Sydney taxis are licensed and cars are inspected regularly. Most take local debit and international credit cards but you can save around 10% by paying cash. All are metered. In the CBD it is generally easier to hail a taxi than call one. Look for a cab with the orange light on and raise

Bike Lockers
Secure bicycle lockers have been installed at some CityRail stations. You can rent one for a minimum period of three months for $50 plus a refundable key deposit of $50. Visit www.bicyclensw.org.au or call 02 9218 5400 for locations.

your arm. You can call a cab (see table - a charge of $1.50 is payable) or you can find ranks at railway stations, major shopping centres, outside big hotels and at Chalmers Street, Chifley Square and Park Street. Changeover is at 03:00 and 15:00 and you may find it more difficult to get a cab at these times. Drivers are allowed to refuse fares as they head back to base. Rates in urban areas are set at $1.68 per kilometre, on top of a $2.90 initial charge. Waiting time is set at 72.17 cents per minute. Luggage charges should never exceed 55 cents. Maxi cabs, for six or more passengers, can charge up to 150% of these fares. Passengers in all taxis are liable for any toll fees.

Taxi Companies

Combined Taxis	13 3300	www.taxiscombined.com.au
Legion Cabs	13 1451	www.legioncabs.com
Premier Cabs	13 1017	www.premiercabs.com.au
RSL Cabs	02 9581 1111	www.rslcabs.com
Silver Service Taxis	13 3100	www.silverservice.com.au
St George Cabs	13 2166	www.stgeorgecabs.com.au
Wheelchair Accessible	1800 043 187	www.zero200.com.au

Train

CityRail (www.cityrail.info, 13 1500) trains service the city, suburbs and out to the Blue Mountains. CountryLink (www.countrylink.info, 13 2232) provides services throughout NSW and direct to Melbourne and Brisbane. Every rail line in Sydney leads directly or indirectly to the City Circle, the underground railway that accesses the CBD and tourist attractions. Trains run every two to three minutes in both directions. There are six stations and a ticket to the city can be used to get on or off at any of these. See inside back cover for the CityRail map. By far the best ticket to buy is the TravelPass. These offer unlimited travel within set zones by bus, train, tram and ferry. Weekly, quarterly and yearly tickets are available. The 'red' zone covers central Sydney and the ferry to Manly, for $33 a week. The 'Day Tripper' allows you to ride the train, bus and ferry all day within the Sydney suburban area for $15.40.

Monorail

The elevated monorail runs through the city, rattling above the streets to Darling Harbour, the Powerhouse Museum and back. To access the Monorail from the city there is a stop on the corner of Pitt and Market Streets. Services run every three to five minutes. Visit www.monorail.com.au or phone 02 9285 5600. Tickets are available from stations, with a standard fare costing $4.50. Children under five go free.

Light Rail

The Light Rail tram connects Sydney's Central station to Haymarket, Paddy's Markets, Darling Harbour Star City, Sydney Fish Market and the city's inner western suburbs. Services run every 10 minutes, night and day, every day. Phone 02 9285 5600 or visit www.monorail.com.au. Tickets are available from customer service officers on the Light Rail itself. Fares start at $3 for a single within one zone. Children under five go free.

Essentials

Places to Stay

From backpacking to multiple-star luxury, Sydney's accommodation options are endless. Expect good quality and old-fashioned Aussie value for money.

Accommodation is spread over the city, but you will find clusters in popular areas like The Rocks, Darling Harbour and the central business district (CBD). The type of accommodation ranges from the ultra-luxurious and modern to dives aimed at spendthrift backpackers. You will find hotel chains, self-catering apartments, boutique hotels, bed and breakfasts, pub stays and budget hostels. Prices vary but there are often special offers and discounts available. These will depend on the time of year and the day of the week. Staying longer usually gets you a better rate and choosing a room without a view will cut costs too. Visit the websites listed to get an idea of what's available.

Your location will depend on what you are looking for in Sydney. If it's sightseeing, The Rocks, Darling Harbour and CBD will all suit well. If you are after the youth scene, head for Kings Cross, Bondi and Manly.

The Dollar Sign

The dollar sign is intended to give a rough idea on costs. These are based on prices in mid 2007 for a double room, and are subject to change.
$ - Under $150
$ $ - $151-$300
$ $ $ - $301+

The view from the Park Hyatt

Sydney *mini* Explorer

Essentials

Places to Stay

Essentials — Places to Stay

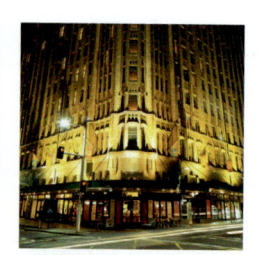

Grace Hotel
www.gracehotel.com.au
02 9272 6888
Built in 1930, this elegantly restored, heritage-listed building is a very comfortable base. The staff are friendly and helpful, the business facilities are good and the rooms are spacious and stylish.
$ $

Hilton
www.hiltonsydney.com.au
02 9266 2000
After a $200 million makeover, the Hilton has won a bundle of awards. The new design feels really light and spacious. You can also dine at the restaurant glass brasserie. See p.165 for more.
$ $ $

The Hughenden
www.hughendenhotel.com.au
1800 642 432
This hotel has 36 authentically restored en-suite rooms. The setting is cosy and intimate, the staff friendly and helpful. Tea is served in the conservatory where a rocking horse and grand piano add to the magic.
$ $ $

Lord Nelson Brewery Hotel
www.lordnelson.com.au
02 9251 4044
This historic pub is set in one of Australia's finest sandstone buildings. There are just nine rooms, they are on the cosy side and you have to negotiate the stairs with your luggage, but it's worth it.
$ $

The Medusa
www.medusa.com.au
02 9331 1000
This heritage-listed Victorian building houses an outrageously quirky boutique hotel. The startling blend of contemporary and heritage works well and has proved a magnet for creatives. There are 18 rooms.
$ $

The Observatory Hotel
www.observatoryhotel.com
02 9256 2222
This award winning hotel drips with colonial opulence and the service is excellent. The hotel's heated pool features a ceiling of fibre optic lights in the outline of the southern hemisphere constellations.
$ $ $

Essentials

Places to Stay

Essentials

Places to Stay

Park Hyatt
www.sydney.park.hyatt.com
02 9241 1234
This hotel is located right under the Harbour Bridge, so it feels as if the Opera House is at the end of your bed. The rooms are airy, modern and sophisticated, and there's a personal butler at your disposal.
$ $ $

Radisson Plaza
www.radisson.com
02 9320 4433
Built in the 19th century and painstakingly restored, this hotel has married old world with mod cons to create an air of chic intimacy. There are a choice of rooms, from presidential on down, and they are all quiet.
$ $

Simpsons of Potts Point
www.simpsonhotel.com
02 9356 2199
The atmosphere is intimate in this meticulously restored hotel, the location is good and there are lovely night views to be enjoyed. The welcome is warm and lots of attention is given to detail.
$

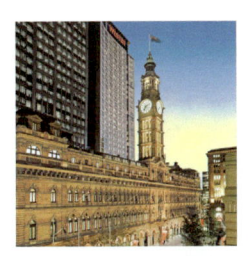

The Westin
www.westin.com
1800 656 535
Absorbed into the historic Sydney General Post Office, the Westin combines light and space with historic atmosphere. The rooms are luxurious and great attention has been given to things like perfect shower fixtures.
$ $

Hotel 59
www.hotel59.com.au
02 9360 5900
A boutique bed and breakfast with a central location. There are only nine rooms, so book ahead. All rooms have a private bathroom and TV, and are air-conditioned. Book online for special discount rates.
$

Hotel Altamont
www.altamont.com.au
02 9360 6000
The Altamont used to be the hangout of celebs like Mick Jagger. Now it offers accommodation at a budget level. Some rooms open onto a private courtyard and there is a guest lounge and rooftop garden.
$

Essentials — Places to Stay

Other Hotels
The hotels listed in the table opposite offer a few other options for places to stay. Here, we've included a few more boutiques that we think are pretty cool, and a few three and five star hotels that we think offer decent value for money.

Hostels
Sydney is something of a backpacker haven, with plenty of places catering to gap year travellers from Europe and young Aussies out to explore their vast backyard. These tend to be clustered around vibey areas such as Kings Cross, Bondi and Manly. They are the cheapest way to stay, typically offering a bunk bed in a dormitory room. Most will also have large common areas, kitchens and laundry facilities. In the popular locations, guests may be limited to a stay of up to seven days.

Hostels

Abbey on King	02 9519 2099	www.theabbeyonking.com.au
Big Hostel	02 9281 6030	www.bighostel.com
Bondi YHA	02 9365 2088	www.yha.com.au
Glebe YHA	02 9692 8418	www.yha.com.au
Globe Backpackers	02 9326 9675	www.globebackpackers.com
Jolly Swagman	02 9358 6400	www.jollyswagman.com.au
Manly Guesthouse	02 9977 0884	www.ozpitality.com.au
Railway Square YHA	02 9281 9666	www.yha.com.au
Sinclairs	02 9371 1149	www.sinclairsbondi.com.au
Sydney Central YHA	02 9218 9000	www.yha.com.au
Wake Up!	02 9288 7888	www.wakeup.com.au

Other Hotels

Five Star

Amora Hotel Jamison	02 9626 2500	www.amorahotels.com.au
Four Points Sheraton	02 9290 4000	www.fourpoints.com
Four Seasons	1800 221 335	www.fourseasons.com
InterContinental	02 9253 9000	www.sydney.intercontinental.com
Novotel	02 9934 0000	www.novotel.com
Shangri-La	02 9250 6000	www.shangri-la.com
Sheraton on the Park	02 9286 6000	www.sheraton.com
Sir Stamford	02 9252 4600	www.stamford.com.au
Sofitel Wentworth	02 9230 0700	www.sofitelsydney.com.au
Swissotel Sydney	02 9238 8888	www.swissotel.com
Sydney Marriott	1800 025 419	www.marriott.com

Three Star

Alfred Park Budget	02 9319 4031	www.alfredpark.com.au
Central Railway	02 9319 7800	www.centralrailwayhotel.com
Glenferrie Lodge	02 9955 1685	www.glenferrielodge.com
Harbour Breeze	02 9181 2420	www.harbourbreezelodge.com
Maze Backpackers	02 9211 5115	www.mazebackpackers.com
Russell Hotel	02 9241 3543	www.therussel.com.au
Sullivans Hotel	02 9361 0211	www.sullivans.com.au
The Crest Hotel	1800 221 805	www.thecresthotel.com.au
The George Hotel	02 9211 1800	www.thegeorge.com.au

Boutique

Blue	02 9331 9000	www.tajhotels.com
Establishment	02 9240 3100	www.merivale.com
Kirketon	02 9332 2011	www.kirketon.com.au
The Australian	02 9247 2229	www.australianheritagehotel.com

Exploring

- **52** Explore Sydney
- **54** At a Glance
- **56** Bondi & Around
- **62** CBD
- **68** Circular Quay & The Rocks
- **74** Darling Harbour & Chinatown
- **80** The Harbour
- **84** Manly
- **90** North Sydney
- **94** Further Out
- **100** Tours & Sightseeing

Exploring

Explore Sydney

Sydney's suburbs each have unique appeal. There's sand and surf to the east, urban sophistication in the middle, convict history around the quay, and the glamour of the harbour itself.

Sydney is a grand mix of the adrenaline pumping and the mind expanding. To get the heart rate up, you can scale the bridge, surf the waves or walk the cliffs. To sate your cerebral yearnings, take in the city's violent past, or the vibrant excitement of its artisitic present.

For most visitors, Sydney begins with Circular Quay and The Rocks. The latter is rich with the history of Australia as a colony and houses the impressive Museum of Contemporary Art (p.70). Walking Tours (p.105) are a good start, and the Susannah Place Museum gives an insight into living conditions at the beginning of the 20th century. And of course, the Opera House (p.69) and Sydney Harbour Bridge (p.68) offer photo ops to rival those of any city in the world. See a show at the former, or stroll across (or over) the latter to get to know them better.

Head south to find the CBD, the heart of Sydney's business world. Here you'll also find its shopping hotspots (p.132), the Art Gallery of NSW and the Sydney museum. It also has two of the city's lovliest green areas; Hyde Park, and the Royal Botanic Gardens and Domain (see p.65).

Kings Cross traffic

Bondi (p.57) and Manly (p.85) are the quintessential Aussie beaches, best known for their surf lifestyle, but each with a distinct feel and crowd.

Sydney's north shore is often missed by tourists and willfully ignored by residents south of the water. But in Taronga Zoo (p.91) it has one of Sydney's gems, and the area around Kirribilli is full of leafy colonial charm.

Back over the water, and to the west of the CBD, lies the recently developed Darling Harbour. The clean up was at first maligned, but the area is now something of an entertainment hub for locals and tourists. It is full of museums, notably the National Maritime Museum (p.75) and Powerhouse Museum (p.75) and has the impressive aquarium (p.76) and Sydney Wildlife World (p.76).

There's a lot to see, so we've divided the city into different areas for you to explore. Now go and find it.

Exploring

Explore Sydney

At A Glance

Exploring

Don't fret about missing out on Sydney's best sandy stretches, museums, natural wonders and wildlife, it's all here, at the turn of a page...

Heritage Sites

Fort Denison	p.80
Manly Quarantine Station	p.86
North Fort	p.84
The Mint	p.65

Museums & Art Galleries

Art Gallery of NSW	p.63
Gavala Aboriginal Art & Cultural Centre	p.74
Manly Art Gallery & Museum	p.84
Museum of Contemporary Art	p.70
Museum of Sydney	p.64
National Maritime Museum	p.75
Powerhouse Museum	p.75
S.H Ervin	p.70
Sussanah Place Museum	p.71

Beaches, Parks & Gardens

Bondi Beach	p.57
Bondi to Bronte Cliff Walk	p.59
Bradfield Park	p.91
Bronte Beach	p.58
Chinese Garden	p.75

Coogee Beach	p.59
Hermitage Walking Track	p.81
Hyde Park	p.62
Lunar Park	p.90
Manly Beach	p.85
Manly Scenic Walk	p.85
Royal Botanic Gardens and Domain	p.65
Shark Island	p.81
Sydney Harbour & National Park	p.81
Tumbalong Park	p.76

Sights & Attractions

Blue Mountains	p.95
Central Coast and Newcastle	p.96
Garrison Church	p.71
Hunter Valley	p.94
Kangaroo Valley	p.97
Oceanworld	p.86
Southern Highlands	p.98
St Mary's Cathedral	p.63
Sydeny Aquarium	p.76
Sydney Harbour Bridge & Pylon Lookout	p.68
Sydney Observatory	p.69
Sydney Opera House	p.69
Sydney Tower	p.64
Sydney WIldlife World	p.76
Taronga Zoo	p.91
Wollongong and Illawarra	p.97

Exploring

Bondi & Around

The eastern suburbs are home to Australia's quintessential surf culture, complete with bronzed lifesavers and the country's most famous beach.

Bondi may well be Sydney's most famous suburb. Home to humble working class apartments from the 1920s to 1950s, frenzied rebuilding and renovating has seen the area change dramatically since the 1990s (and prices skyrocket accordingly). The well-preserved 1920s Bondi Pavilion gives you a taste of what Bondi used to look like but these days the seaside suburb is a thriving mix of pale backpackers, topless teenagers, body builders, media types and the odd international celebrity. If you're planning on going swimming be wary of the southern end, which can have a strong riptide (dubbed 'the backpacker express').

The main street, Campbell Parade, has everything from basic takeaways, cafes and ice-cream parlours to fine dining, tacky souvenirs and trendy street clothes. The best shopping is on Gould Street, an up-and-coming fashion precinct with trendy shops like Tuchuzy (see

Emergency Rescue

The strong currents off Bondi can be very dangerous. If you get into difficulty when swimming, don't panic – fighting against a current will only tire you out. Just float with it, breathe evenly, keep your head above water and raise one arm to signal the lifeguards. Always swim between the flags.

p.132) and One Teaspoon (see p.132), and the upmarket Westfield Bondi Junction (p.140) is large enough to get lost in for a day. Better for bargains are the massive Bondi markets (see p.136), held every Sunday. Those looking for beachwear have their pick of the best in Bondi, with everything you need available all year round (see p.144 for more).

For drinks with a view, the Bondi Social (p.159) and North Bondi RSL are hard to beat (get in early to grab an outdoor table), while on the southern end the bistro at Icebergs is a cheaper alternative to the famous see-and-be-seen restaurant above (see p.159 for a review).

For food, fight for a coveted window seat at Trio Café (02 9365 6044) on Campbell Parade or wile away a rainy day at Gertrude and Alice (p.159), which has second-hand books to browse through over coffee. Green's Cafe on Glenayr Avenue is the local's haunt, as it has good home-cooked fare away from the touristy main strip. From Bondi you can walk to Coogee or Bronte along the well-trodden cliff-edge path for stunning views (see p.59). Just remember to wear sunscreen when you're on the beach, and, where possible, avoid the sun completely between 11:00 and 14:00, particularly in summer.

*For **restaurants and bars** in the area, see p.158. For **shopping**, see Bondi Markets (p.136) and Beachwear (p.144)*

Bondi Beach
Bondi

The most famous of Australia's beaches, no other strip of sand has the same allure. Its mile-long curved expanse of white sand looks even more impressive viewed from the southern hill above the beach. Surfers tend to stick to the southern end where the rocks kick up the waves; the centre is dominated by sunbathers; while families tend to fill up the northern end near the free shallow salt-water pool. Bondi (pronounced bon-dye) is protected by shark nets and there are two sets of flags for swimmers and boogie boarders. The Bondi Pavilion has toilets, showers and changing rooms plus a basic kiosk. If you're looking for more satisfying sustenance, Campbell Parade is packed with cafes, ice-cream and fish 'n' chip shops and fine dining restaurants. The bustling carnival-like atmosphere makes it popular with locals and visitors alike.

Bondi Junction and 333, Map p.239 F2

Bronte Beach
Bronte

Much smaller and less image conscious than Bondi, the family-oriented Bronte has an excellent shady beachside park; perfect for kicking a ball and popular for picnics. The rolling surf can be rough here so steer clear of the rocks at either end. To play it safe, stick to the Bronte Baths, an enclosed free-access pool at the southern end of the beach. Locals converge on the cafe-lined hill to soak up some sun over brunch or bake on the beach where Norfolk pines offer some shade. The mini train ($3) and playground are a big hit with the tiny tots. From here, you can walk north to Bondi or south to Clovelly via the historic Waverley Cemetery, which sits on a headland with incredible ocean views.

Bondi Junction and 360/361/378

Tamarama Beach
02 9300 9056
Dellview St, between Bondi & Bronte Beach
This tiny beach attracts similarly uber-cool beach lovers as Bondi and Bronte, but far fewer tourists. Popular with the gay crowd, the bodies here are likely to be the most buffed and bronzed in all of Sydney. The park on the beach is a great spot for an Aussie barbecue but it doesn't offer much shade. Despite the peaceful appearance of this cosy cove, be wary of rip tides, particularly near the rocks at either end of the beach. Surfing is prohibited. Bondi Junction and 381, Map p.239 E4 **2**

Bondi to Bronte Cliff Walk
Begins at Bondi Baths
Down at the southern end of Bondi beach, next to the pool and Icebergs Club (p.117) begins the Bondi to Bronte walk. This 2.5 km cliff path takes in all the beaches mentioned above on a one hour stroll.
Bondi Junction and 333, Map p.239 E2 **22**

Coogee Beach
Coogee
Pronounced kuh-jee, this is another safe swimming spot if you don't like big waves or have kids in tow. The area has been greened up by the council and now boasts a playground on the grassy headland overlooking the beach. Big kids are more likely to be attracted by the Coogee Bay Hotel, where the oceanfront balcony is a popular backpacker drinking spot and often hosts excellent live bands. There's a cosy, community feel to this area. Bondi Junction and 314

Exploring

If you only do one thing in...
Bondi & Around

Have a crack at surfing Bondi (p.57), Sydney's world famous beach.

Best for...

Eating: For the best brekkie in town, it has to be Macro Wholefoods Café (see p.160).

Drinking: The million-dollar views and the extensive winelist at Icebergs Dining Room and Bar (see p.159) make this a memorable dining experience.

Sightseeing: Take a snap of the iconic Bondi lifesavers in their natty red and yellow outfits (p.57).

Shopping: Bondi's Campbell Parade has lots of trendy surf shops (see p.132).

Outdoor: The hour-long stroll from Bondi to Bronte offers some breathtaking scenery (see p.59).

Exploring

CBD

Sydney's bustling business heartland comes with a bounty of shops, sights and rolling green spaces.

The bustling Central Business District stretches from Circular Quay to just beyond Town Hall. At its core is Martin Place, the financial heartland of Sydney. It's also a great place to spend money, with the Pitt Street Mall, the Strand Arcade and the Queen Victoria Building all here. It is also home to the city's two lovliest green spaces - Hyde Park (below) and The Domain, and an interesting array of churches and museums. *For restaurants and bars in the area, see p.162. For shopping, see p.139.*

Hyde Park
CBD

02 9265 9550
www.cityofsydney.nsw.gov.au

Lying at the edge of the city's business district, this grassy expanse was first declared public land by Governor Phillip in 1792 and used for cricket matches and horse races. These days it's packed with sun-seeking city workers on their lunch hour. The magnificent avenue of Moreton Bay figs is particularly pretty at night, when it's illuminated with fairy lights. At the southern end stands a 30m high art deco ANZAC memorial, erected in 1934 to commemorate Australians killed at war – the 120,000 gold stars inside the dome represent each man and woman of NSW who served. You can't miss the grand bronze and granite Archibald Fountain, which was built in 1932 to commemorate the French and Australian first world war alliance. Museum or St James, Map p.234 B4

St Mary's Cathedral

02 9220 0400

Cnr College & Cathedral Sts   www.sydney.catholic.org.au

The original St Mary's catholic church was destroyed by fire in 1865 and rebuilt in 1886. The twin spires you see today were added at a cost of $8 million in 2000 to match the original plans drawn up by William Wardell in 1865. Notable features include the large rose window and the terrazzo floor in the crypt, which shows the six days of creation. This grand building is quite a prominent landmark, sitting just over the road from Hyde Park and marking the entrance to Art Gallery Road and The Domain. It is also the seat of the archbishop of Sydney. The cathedral is open from Monday to Friday, 06:30-18:30 and Saturday 08:00-18:30. There are tours on Sundays at midday. St James, Map p.234 B3

Art Gallery of NSW

02 9225 1744

Art Gallery Rd, The Domain   www.artgallery.nsw.gov.au

The gallery houses three floors of Australian, Asian, European and contemporary art, including works by big Aussie names like Arthur Streeton and Brett Whiteley. Don't miss the Asian art section in the glass light box facing Woolloomooloo. There's an excellent collection of works by Aborigines and Torres Strait Islanders on level one, where the canteen has gorgeous water views (open daily, 10:00-16:30, with evening dining on Wednesdays until 20:30). Three hours will only scratch the surface of what this large gallery has to offer. General admission is free (except for special exhibitions); open from 10:00-17:00 and until 21:00 on Wednesdays.

St James, Map p.234 C3

Sydney **mini** Explorer

Museum of Sydney
02 9251 5988
Cnr Phillip & Bridge Sts
www.hht.net.au

If you're interested in Sydney's short but colourful history, this will be a highlight on your museum itinerary. The objects, pictures and multimedia exhibitions detail early settlement from 1788, including some Aboriginal history. Built on the foundations of the first Government House, thousands of artefacts found here in archaeological digs are on display. There's a good cafe next door with free newspapers. Allow two hours. Open daily, 09:30-17:00. Adult $10, child $5, concession $20. Wheelchair access.

Circular Quay, Map p.234 B1 6

Sydney Tower
02 9333 9222
100 Market St
www.skywalk.com.au

Adrenalin junkies might not feel an almighty rush, but seeing Sydney from the outdoor platform is still more exciting than surveying the skyline from behind glass. Only open since 2005, the views from up here are spectacular, and at 260m it's almost double the height of the Harbour Bridge. If you feel queasy, try not to chunder over the safety ledge as you'll be fined $5,000. You're harnessed to safety railings the whole time and the guides let you in on interesting city secrets – like the snipers allegedly stationed on the balcony of the US embassy since September 2001. Admission includes access to the observation deck and OzTrek, a goofy simulated ride through Australia on 180 degree screens. Open from 09:00-00:15. Adult $109, child $85 (must be 10 years or older).

St James, Map p.234 A4 23

The Mint
10 Macquarie St

02 8239 2288
www.hht.net.au

Constructed over five years from 1811, when NSW settlers first struck gold, the Mint was built as the southern wing of the Sydney Hospital. It was converted to a mint in 1854 (the first Royal Mint outside of England) with a sandstone coining factory built out the back. It operated until 1926, when the Mint was shifted to the nation's new capital, Canberra. The small museum has closed but the building itself is worth a look. Open Monday to Friday, 09:00-17:00. Free admission.

Martin Place, Map p.234 B3

Royal Botanic Gardens & Domain
The Domain

02 9231 8111
www.rbgsyd.nsw.gov.au

This beautiful green expanse with ponds and flourishing flowerbeds is as much loved by locals as tourists. Its initial function was less aesthetic. Settlers used this spot as a giant veggie patch, but it failed to feed the hungry hordes due to poor soil. A great spot for panoramic harbour views is Mrs Macquarie's Chair, a peninsula named after a governor's wife, Elizabeth Macquarie. Legend has it that if a woman sitting here makes a wish it will come true. Keep an eye out for magpies and, if you're here around dusk, the hordes of fruit bats that flock to the gardens. Open daily from 07:00 to sunset. There are free 90-minute guided tours each day at 10:30 and a one-hour tour at 13:00; both depart from the Palm Grove Centre. Aboriginal heritage tours depart at 14:00 ($20), from the Moore Room. Martin Place, Map p.234 C1

Sydney **mini** Explorer

Exploring

If you only do one thing in...
CBD

Take a leisurely stroll through the Moreton Bay fig trees in Hyde Park (p.62).

Best for...

Eating: Celebrity restauranteur Luke Mangan has created one of Sydney's hippest spots, glass brasserie (p.165), at the Hilton.

Drinking: Purple Sneakers (p.167) is all packed dance floors, sweaty bodies and a house party vibe, with a cover charge of just $10.

Sightseeing: St Mary's cathedral (p.63) and the Museum of Sydney (p.64) should not be missed.

Shopping: Pitt Street Mall (p.139) is the heart of Sydney's shopping district.

Outdoor: The Royal Botanic Gardens (p.65) are a pretty, tranquil way to escape the bustle of the city.

Circular Quay & The Rocks

This is the part of town that no visitor misses. Sydney's two glamorous icons sit on either side and the city's grim early history lies within.

Framed by the Harbour Bridge and Opera House, this heritage-rich area is often the first port of call for visitors. In the 19th century, The Rocks was renowned as a place of debauchery; it's claimed you could hear the noise of the gambling houses and opium dens a mile offshore. When the bubonic plague hit in 1900, the government bought the area and demolished parts of it in an attempt to control the spread of disease. It was largely abandoned until the 1970s, when a clean-up operation began that created the tourist hotspot it is today. See p.105 for walking tours. *For **restaurants and bars** in the area, see p.170. For **shopping**, see Hotspots, p.134*

Sydney Harbour Bridge & Pylon Lookout
The Rocks

02 9240 1100
www.pylonlookout.com.au

Sydney's iconic 'coathanger' was a massive engineering feat for its time and still impresses today. You can walk across for free (south bank access is from Cumberland Street), or climb the 200 steps of the south east pylon for $9.50 (children $3.50, under 7s free, open 10:00-17:00 daily). You get fabulous harbour views and there is also a three-level exhibit of the bridge's history. Braver visitors may want to climb the famous arch (www.bridgeclimb.com / 8274 7777). It's not cheap, but gives spectacular views of the harbour 134m below. Guided tours run every 10 minutes on most days. It's a one-hour climb up 1,439 steps, so you'll have plenty of time to enjoy the view. You can't take your camera so you'll have to fork out extra for a personal photo (the group photo is free). Monday to Friday $169-$200. Twilight tour $249-$260, exclusive dawn tour $295, first Saturday of every month. Groups leave from 5 Cumberland Street. Circular Quay, Map p.226 C1 24

Sydney Observatory 02 9241 3767
Observatory Hill, The Rocks   www.sydneyobservatory.com.au

This impressive dome-topped 1850s building covers astronomy from two distinct points of view; modern science and Aboriginal sky stories. Night tours, which must be pre-booked, offer the chance to view the sky through a telescope and learn about the Southern Cross. The hill itself is a very pleasant spot to spend a few idle hours. Open daily 10:00-17:00. Free admission to gardens and museum. Night tours; adults $15, child $10, concession $12, family $45.
 Circular Quay, Map p.226 A3 9

Sydney Opera House 02 9250 7111
Bennelong Pt, Circular Quay   www.sydneyoperahouse.com

The Sydney Opera House opened in 1973, 16 years after Danish architect Joern Utzon won a competition with his dramatic design. Legend has it that his was plucked from the rejects pile by one of the judges. His luck didn't last though. After budget blowouts and political wrangling, Utzon resigned in 1966, and a team of Australian architects finished the job. Critics point out that all the attention went on the majestic exterior, resulting in less-than-perfect acoustics inside. Open 09:00-17:00. The one-hour tours go every half hour. Adult $26, concession $16, online bookings $23. A two hour backstage tour leaves at 07:00 and costs $140 (no kids), includes breakfast. Circular Quay, Map p.227 F2 10

Museum of Contemporary Art
02 9245 2400
140 George St, The Rocks   www.mca.com.au

This striking building is a must-do if you're interested in 19th and 20th century art. Sitting right on Circular Quay, it has been home to more than 5,000 pieces by Australian and international artists since 1991. Works from the 1960s onwards are on display, including significant contemporary Aboriginal collections. Allow two hours for a visit. Open daily, 10:00-17:00. Wheelchair access. With an outside terrace overlooking the harbour, the MCA Cafe is a popular spot for lingering. For reservations, call 9241 4253. More spectacular still is the view from the Harbour Terrace on level five, which is often booked for functions. Circular Quay, Map p.226 C3 11

S.H. Ervin
02 9258 0173
National Trust, Watson Rd   www.nsw.nationaltrust.org.au

The hundreds of paintings that don't make it into the coveted Archibald Prize exhibition at the Art Gallery of NSW can be seen here at the Salon des Refusés; an alternative exhibition jokingly dubbed 'The Archibald Rejects'. It took its name from the original Salon des Refusés, which was staged by Napoleon in Paris in 1863 for those artists whose works had been refused by the official Salon – including Cézanne and Manet. Talks are held every Sunday at 15:00 (free with exhibition entry). The 1856 building was once part of a school, but is now the headquarters of the National Trust. They host seven exhibitions of Australian art each year. Open 11:00-17:00 Tuesday to Sunday. Admission $6. Circular Quay, Map p.226 A4 **25**

Garrison Church
02 9247 1268
Cnr Argyle & Lower Fort Sts   www.thegarrisonchurch.org.au

Officially named Holy Trinity and set in The Rocks, Sydney's oldest church became known as the Garrison because military regiments worshipped here after the foundation stone was laid in 1840. Stone was used from the Argyle cut, so the church was quarried from its immediate surroundings. Notable features include the brilliantly coloured east window and the carved red cedar pulpit. It has a small museum featuring historical and military items. Open 09:00-17:00 daily. Free admission. Circular Quay, Map p.224 B3

Susannah Place Museum
02 9241 1893
58-64 Gloucester St   www.hht.nsw.gov.au

Inside this row of four tiny terrace houses is a time capsule. Here you'll discover what the living conditions were like for some of the local working class of the 1900s. The curators are dressed for the part but the tour through the old kitchens, laundries and dunnies is virtually self-guided. You can purchase replica wares from the recreated 1959 corner store. Open Saturday and Sunday from 10:00-17:00. Adult $8, child $4, family $17. Circular Quay, Map p.226 B3 **12**

Exploring

If you only do one thing in...
Circular Quay & The Rocks

Stroll through the Rocks to the Pylon Lookout (p.68).

Best for...

Eating: Get along to Guillaume at Bennelong, for mod Oz with a classical French influence under the shadow of the Opera House (p.69).

Drinking: Try one of more than 300 cocktails up on the 36th floor of the Shangri-La Hotel at the The Blu Horizon Bar (p.171).

Sightseeing: Hop on the Manly ferry from Wharf 3 (see p.103) for a pleasure cruise that will top any sightseeing tour at a fraction of the cost.

Shopping: Browse the stores for some authentic Aboriginal artwork, or an original piece by one of Australia's favourite artists (see p.134).

Outdoor: Rest up in the shadows of the Sydey Harbour Bridge on Observatory Hill (p.69).

Exploring

Darling Harbour & Chinatown

This brash entertainment hub mixes culture, history, eating and drinking with a vast casino, souvenir shops, pleasant parks and pretty little walkways.

The once dilapidated shipping docks at Darling Harbour are now an entertainment precinct. Redeveloped for Australia's bicentenary in 1988, millions of dollars were spent building the little used Monorail and the Harbourside Shopping Centre. The area had little to offer locals until relatively recently when swish bars and restaurants opened at Cockle Bay and King Street Wharves. Nearby Chinatown is an authentic slice of Asia with bustling markets, fresh yum cha and exotic Asian groceries.
*For **restaurants and bars** in the area, see p.174. For **shopping**, see Paddy's Market, p.137.*

Gavala Aboriginal Art & Cultural Centre   02 9212 7232
Harbourside Centre, Darling Harbour   www.gavala.com.au

This is Sydney's only gallery dedicated to indigenous art, with an extensive collection of modern and traditional styles. The exhibition space has a shop, so you can take home authentic Aboriginal artworks. Choose from iconic boomerangs, masks, statues and ceremonial jewellery. These pieces are a step above the Australiana found in souvenir shops. Keanu Reeves, Prince Harry and The Red Hot Chili Peppers have all stopped by to snap up a hand-painted didgeridoo. Open 10:00-21:00 daily. Wheelchair access.   Harbourside, Map p.231 D3 29

National Maritime Museum   02 9298 3777
2 Murray St, Darling Harbour   www.anmm.gov.au

This museum is easy to spot thanks to its white, sail-like roof. It explains Australia's long relationship with the sea, including everything from beach culture to Aboriginal fishing methods. If you're planning to explore the ships moored outside, allow at least two hours here. Open daily 09.30-17:00. The permanent indoor gallery is free. Guided tours from 10:00-14:00. Wheelchair access. Harbourside, Map p.231 D3 **13**

Powerhouse Museum   02 9217 0111
500 Harris St, Darling Harbour   www.powerhousemuseum.com

Science buff or not, the thought-provoking exhibits at The Powerhouse are fun. Even without dawdling, it would take days to see them all. Highlights include the world's oldest steam engine and the Strasbourg Clock, a working model of the astronomical clock in Strasbourg's Notre Dame cathedral. Allow at least three hours. Open from 10:00-17:00 daily. Adult $10, child $5, concession $6, family $25. Free for under 5s and over 55s. Wheelchair access. Haymarket, Map p.233 D2 **14**

Chinese Garden   02 9281 6863
Darling Harbour   www.chinesegarden.com.au

Created for the bicentenary in 1998, this Chinese-designed garden is a tranquil escape from the crowds at Darling Harbour. The winding pathways take you past ponds blooming with lotus flowers, mini waterfalls and statues. Adult $6, child/concession $3, family $15.

Garden Plaza, Map p.233 E1 **15**

Tumbalong Park
Darling Harbour

A little patch of greenery among Darling Harbour's concrete, this small park often has live entertainment and concerts. The free playground and timed acrobatic water features means it's mostly used by families, but it's also a good place for weary shoppers to set down their bags.

Garden Plaza, Map p.233 D1 **16**

Sydney Aquarium
02 8251 7800
Aquarium Pier, Darling Harbour   www.sydneyaquarium.com.au

Highlights here include penguins, seals and sharks frolicking around the fibreglass tunnels, the glass-bottomed walkway (the closest you'll ever come to walking on water) and the tropical fish in the Great Barrier Reef section. Up to 5,000 people visit here each week and a visit is well worth the steep entry fee. Open daily 09:00-22:00. Adult $26, child $13.50, family $42-$63. Darling Park, Map p.231 E3 **17**

Sydney Wildlife World
02 9333 9288
Aquarium Pier   www.sydneywildlifeworld.com.au

Come here for a beautiful butterfly enclosure, cute marsupials and scary spiders and snakes. You can't touch the wallabies or koalas but you can watch them go about their business in the glass enclosure. Don't be alarmed to see snakes or lizards outside their enclosures; roaming rangers have them slinked across their shoulders so you can get up close and personal (10:00-17:00). Open daily, 09:00-22:00. Adult $27.10, child $13.80, family $64.60. Darling Park, Map p.231 E3 **26**

Darling Harbour at night

Exploring

Darling Harbour & Chinatown

Exploring

If you only do one thing in...
Darling Harbour & Chinatown

Walk among the sharks at Sydney Aquarium (p.76).

Best for...

Eating: Even at full capacity, the service at the Ice Cube Seafood Grill Bar (p.176) is as slick as the interior.

Drinking: Sink into leather loungers while surrounded by beautiful people at the Loft Bar (p.176).

Sightseeing: See a menagere of Australia's cutest creatures at the Sydney Wildlife World (p.76).

Shopping: For the tackiest Australiana in town, head to Harbourside shopping centre. See map, p.231, D3.

Outdoor: Find a state of meditative calm at the Chinese Garden (p.75).

Exploring

The Harbour

Sydney's harbour is the city's defining feature and provides what may be one of the most beautiful natural settings of any city in the world.

Sydneysiders like to take advantage of their glorious natural surroundings, and the harbour, with its protected outcrops of land, provides a clean, blue and green wilderness, moments from the city. Getting on to the water is as easy as getting a train, and your options are varied. See Boat Tours (p.102), or turn to the Sports and Spas chapter for details on sailing (p.113) excursions or kayaking (p.113).

Fort Denison
Sydney Harbour

02 9247 5033
www.npws.nsw.gov.au

This is where convicts who committed petty crimes were kept in the early days of settlement. Built from 8,000 tonnes of sandstone, it was named after Sir William Denison, then Governor of NSW. The fort's canons are still fired daily at 13:00. The excellent Blue Rock Café (licensed) is surprisingly affordable with great harbour views, or you can picnic on the lawn. There are guided tours, departing from Cadman's Cottage, 110 George Street, Monday to Friday, 11:45-15:00; Saturday to Sunday 11:30-15:00 and 14:30-15:15. (Adults $22, child $18, family $72). They also offer catered brunch tours on Saturdays and Sundays from 09:00-11:40 ($47 adult, $43 child). Map p.225 D3

Shark Island
Off Rose Bay, Sydney Harbour

02 9247 5033
www.npws.nsw.gov.au

This tiny island has a sandy beach, shelter and good picnic facilities. There's no shop but drinking water is available. A return ticket costs $16 for adults, $13.50 for children and $14.50 concession. A family rate of $56 is also available. Bookings can be made through NPWS Information Centre at Cadmans Cottage, The Rocks (number above) or by calling Matilda Cruises on 9264 7377. Map p.225 E3

Hermitage Walking Track
Bay View Hill Rd, Rose Bay

02 9247 5033
www.npws.nsw.gov.au

Less busy than the Bondi to Bronte walk is the Hermitage Walking Track, which has spectacular ocean views. It starts from Bay View Hill Road between the imposing Kambala School and Rose Bay Convent, and takes you via some lovely swimming spots to Nielsen Park, in about one hour. Milk Beach, about halfway along, is likely to be deserted and has views of the bridge in the distance. 324 / 325, Map p.225 E3

Sydney Harbour National Park
Around the harbour

02 9247 5033
www.npws.nsw.gov.au

This national park covers a number of areas dotted about the harbour. The biggest is the large green expanse south of Manly and North Head, where the harbour meets the sea. It also covers Nielsen Park, which is the end of the Hermitage Walking Track (see above) and Bradleys Head, where the park backs on to Taronga Zoo. No visit to the city would be complete without a few hours exploring these areas.

Exploring — The Harbour

Exploring

If you only do one thing in...
The Harbour

Make the most of a city at the water's edge by jumping in a kayak and paddling past the Opera House and under the harbour bridge... (see p.113).

Best for...

Families: Take in the sights on a boat trip and save tired little legs from a few hours walking, see p.102 for Boat Tours.

Relaxing: Pack up a picnic and hop on a ferry out to Shark Island (p.81) for a tranquil day on a secluded beach.

Culture: Take a guided tour of Fort Denison (p.80) for a taste of some local history.

Outdoor: Get out there and active and spend a few hours getting some fresh air in the Sydney Harbour National Park (see p.81).

Sightseeing: The Hermitage Walking Track (p.81) offers some spectacular photo opportunities.

Manly

Manly battles with Bondi as the capital of Sydney's surf culture, and is surrounded by spectacular cliffs and sumptuous walks.

Manly was given its name by Captain Arthur Phillip after seeing the butch physique of the Aborigines in 1788. The locals today may be blonder, but the term still applies. This is Sydney's other surf capital. Although (slightly) less well known than Bondi, it's bars, beaches and natural scenery are just as impressive.
*For **restaurants and bars** in the area, see p.184.*

North Fort
North Head, Scenic Drive

02 9247 5033
www.northfort.org.au

This fort was built in 1934, for fear of a naval attack from Japan. The guided tours allow you to explore the maze of tunnels (bring a torch so you can see) or check out the ancient guns at the National Artillery Museum. There's an onsite cafe with stunning water views as well as picnic grounds surrounded by bushland. Tours are held on the fourth Sunday of every month at 10:30 (adult $39, child $29, including lunch). Manly Ferry Wharf and 135, Map p.225 F2

Manly Art Gallery & Museum
West Esplanade

02 9976 1420
www.manlyweb.com.au

This small gallery celebrates the beach suburb's sun, surf and sand obsession and an insight into the area's beach culture. It also houses an eclectic mix of temporary exhibitions, which range from local quilting artists and student projects to indigenous artworks sourced from central Australia. Open Tuesday to Sunday 10:00-17:00. Adult $3.60, child $1.20. Free on Wednesdays. Manly Ferry Wharf, Map p.243 A2 **27**

Manly Beach
Manly

The atmosphere at this popular beach changes depending on what time of day you arrive. In the early morning and evening, joggers make the most of the long tree-lined walkway above the beach. During the day, it's full of yummy mummies pushing prams and walking their dogs. Beach volleyball games are popular at twilight and outside of working hours it's jam-packed with families, teenagers and tourists. Locals tend to swim at Queenscliff beach at the very northern end of Manly, while snorkellers stick to the rocky area near Shelley Beach. For lunch, fresh fish 'n' chips is a popular meal (the Manly Fish Market & Café on Wentworth Street is excellent) but there are plenty of fast food options. Parking directly on the beach is expensive. Manly Ferry Wharf, Map p.242 C2 **18**

Manly Scenic Walk   02 9247 5033
Sydney Harbour National Park   www.nationalparks.nsw.gov.au

The 9km Manly Scenic Walkway is a well-marked trail that passes through some excellent swimming spots. Running from the Harbour Bridge to Manly, the whole stroll can take five hours. Many choose to cut out the first bit, and walk from the Spit Bridge to Manly, which takes closer to two hours. Catch a 480 bus from North Sydney station to the Spit and begin your walk there. Signs on the north side of the bridge mark the way. This takes you through some dramatic scenery, as you yomp up cliffs to the haven of Manly, with its beach, bars and restaurants. 🚇 North Sydney and 🚌 480, Map p.242 A2 **28**

Oceanworld
02 8251 7877
Manly Cove Beach   www.oceanworld.com.au

More intimate than the Sydney Aquarium, there isn't as much to see but you do get the chance to get involved. If you've ever wanted to touch a python or dive with sharks, this is the place. You can also watch the sharks and massive stingrays being fed by divers, from the fibreglass viewing tunnel at 11:00 on Monday, Wednesday and Friday. Visit after 15:00 to avoid school groups. Adult $17.95, child $9.50, concession $12.95, family $43.95. You get 15% off the ticket price after 15:30. 🚇 Manly Ferry Wharf, Map p.242 A2 **19**

Manly Quarantine Station
1300 886 875
Manly   www.manlyquarantine.com

Tour the cemeteries, isolation wards and mortuary by lantern light and be spooked by the bizarre stories in this history-steeped station. This is where poorly new arrivals were held in a bid to contain smallpox and other deadly diseases. Keep an eye out for the hundreds of wall etchings by former inhabitants. The two hour history tour runs from Wednesday to Friday at 15:00, and on Saturday and Sunday at 10:00 and 15:00. Adult $25, concession $19. Ghost tours run Thursday and Friday at 18:30. Tickets $34 (must be 16 years or over). Family ghost tours run Wednesday to Sunday at 20:00. Adult $25, concession $15. 🚇 Manly Ferry Wharf and 🚌 135, Map p.225 F1

Manly | Exploring

Sydney **mini** Explorer

Exploring

If you only do one thing in...
Manly

Avoid the overland route, and get there by ferry (see p.103 for how).

Best for...

Eating: Flamboyant flamenco, a lively atmosphere and mouthwatering Moroccan and Spanish fare mean the Alhambra Café and Tapas Bar (p.185) is one stop that definitely has to be made.

Drinking: The wide open doors of the Manly Wharf Hotel offer the perfect invitation for a few lazy beers once you hop off the ferry (see p.187).

Sightseeing: Take a spot of lunch with the sharks at Oceanworld (see p.86).

Shopping: Stroll along The Corso for surfwear and tacky Australiana. See map p.242 B2.

Outdoor: The Spit to Manly walk offer views that should not be missed (p.85).

Exploring

North Sydney

Sydney's north shore is home to the Australian Prime Minister and considered distinctly 'old money.' It is a place of rolling green clifftops and colonial grandeur.

Once you cross the Harbour Bridge, the suburbs become leafier and more quiet. While many locals consider the north a little humdrum, it has some gorgeous waterfront spots, particularly at Kirribilli and Cremorne Point. Though not accessible to the public, two colonial mansions at the bottom of Kirribilli can be seen from passing ferries. Kirribilli House is home to the PM and the Governor General (the UK's representative in Australia) lives at Admiralty House, next door. The Kirribilli markets (fourth Saturday of the month) are certainly worth a visit if you're in town, for their antiques, jewellery and retro clothes.

*For **restaurants and bars** in the area, see p.192.*

Luna Park
Olympic Place, Milsons Pt   02 9922 6644   www.lunaparksydney.com.au

This is Sydney's last remaining theme park and behind the laughing face that marks its entrance lies a rocky history. It has been shut down many times, due to financial problems, friction with local residents and a fire in 1979 that killed seven people. It still retains some of its 1930s flavour and the panoramic views of the harbour and city from the ferris wheel are worth the trip. Open Monday and Thursday 11:00-18:00; Friday 11:00-23:00; Saturday 10:00-23:00; Sunday 10:00-18:00. Free admission. Individual rides $6; unlimited ride day pass

$39, child $18-$29 depending on height. Ulimited rides for $25 after 17:00 on Fridays. Milsons Point, Map p.240 A3 20

Taronga Zoo 02 9969 2777
Bradley's Head Rd, Mosman www.zoo.nsw.gov.au

Before the zoo opened in 1916, all the animals, including the elephants, had to be moved from their existing home at Moore Park on a massive barge. Since then there have been several expansions and it now houses 2,600 animals and a new tropical elephant enclosure. Locals love Taronga as much for its stunning harbour views as for the exotic animals. There are daily photo opportunities with giraffes (13:45-14:15) or koalas (11:00-15:00) and regular wildlife shows. You can also camp overnight if you call ahead. A zoo pass from Circular Quay will cover the ferry, cable car and entry fee. Otherwise its adults $32, children $17.50 or $84 for a family. Open 09:00-17:00 daily. Circular Quay and 247

Bradfield Park
Alfred St, Milsons Point www.northsydney.nsw.gov.au

This snaking patch of green wraps itself alongside a string of office blocks before ducking under the bridge and down towards Kirribilli Point. It is a pleasant spot to stroll through and has a footpath that runs west all the way round Lavender Bay, and east to Mary Booth Lookout. This has gorgeous views out over the harbour and to the city opposite and is a favourite for those looking for a different angle for their snaps of the coathanger. It's also popular for watching sailing events and fireworks over the harbour. Milsons Point, Map p.240 B3 21

Exploring

If you only do one thing in...
North Sydney

Take the weight off with a view over the harbour from Mary Booth lookout (p.91).

Best for...

Eating: For a romantic evening over some fabulous Thai-inspired dishes, Nu's restaurant (02 9954 1780) on Blue's Point Road won't disappoint.

Drinking: Do lunch in Plonk! Beach Café in Mosman (02 9960 1007) - the kids will enjoy playing on the nearby stretch of sand as you devour heavenly deserts over a fine glass of wine.

Sightseeing: Have a gawp at the Prime Minister's home from a ferry passing Kirribilli House (p.90).

Shopping: Take in the Kirribilli markets on the fourth Saturday of the month (p.90) or the malls by North Sydney station.

Outdoor: Now's your chance to catch a roo and a croc up close - prepare to marvel at the delights of Taronga Zoo (p.91).

Exploring

Further Out

Within an hour of Circular Quay, city gives way to bush. The Australian relationship with the country's harsh but beautiful nature is imbedded in the national psyche. Get exploring to find out why.

Although there's plenty to keep you occupied in Sydney, you'll get a better sense of the real Australia if you head out into the country. There are many spots near the city; the picturesque Blue Mountains are a welcome relief from Sydney's heat, while the north and south coast have stunning beaches and a laid-back atmosphere. For wine buffs, the Hunter Valley is a must-do while the less touristy Southern Highlands also have an emerging food and wine industry.

Cellar Street

The majority of cellar doors are clustered along Broke Road and Hermitage Road – bike tours are increasingly popular (www.grape mobile.com.au) although some of the narrow, potholed roads may leave you a little saddle sore.

Hunter Valley

New South Wales' best-known wine region, the Hunter Valley is famous for its citrusy semillion and earthy shiraz and has a growing reputation for its olives. As well as free wine tasting, Sydneysiders come here to sample local produce at sophisticated restaurants and pamper themselves at luxury resorts and spa retreats like The Golden Door (4993 8500, www.goldendoor.com.au).

The majority of Hunter Valley wineries are boutique and many only sell their wine through local restaurants or at cellar doors (most open daily from 10:00-17:00). Large wineries like Tyrells (02 9889 4450, www.tyrells.com.au), McWilliams Mt Pleasant (4998 7505, www.mcwilliams.com.au), Drayton's (02 4998 7513, www.draytonswines.com.au) and Wyndham Estate (4938 3444, www.wyndhamestate.com) offer guided tours. At family-run cellar doors like Ernest Hill (02 4991 4418, www.ernesthillwines.com.au), it's often the winemaker filling the glasses. Don't miss Audrey Wilkinson, which was one of the first wineries in the area and has great views over the valley (02 4998 7411, www.audreywilkinson.com.au).

You can pick up a Hunter Valley Wine Country Visitors Guide with a good pullout map from the Visitors Information Centre next to Cessnock Airport (02 4990 0900 or www.winecountry.com.au). For an overnight stay, try Harrigan's Irish Pub & Accomodation (02 4998 4000) or Cypress Lakes Resort (02 4993 1555).

Blue Mountains

Some 120km west of Sydney, the Blue Mountains really do look a hazy blue from a distance; the colour is caused by the evaporation of oil from millions of eucalyptus trees. An ancient seabed that rose over eons and slowly eroded, the Blue Mountains became a World Heritage Site in 2000. The 1,000m high mountains posed a severe obstacle to early settlers until explorers Wentworth, Blaxland and Lawson managed to forge a path along the steep cliffs and canyons in 1813. Today's Great Western Highway still follows the same route, though the Bells Line of Road is a more scenic drive. The Blue Mountains are a particularly popular winter getaway as it often snows in June, July and August. The Carrington Hotel (02 4782 1111) and Lillianfels Blue Mountains Resort & Spa (02 4780 1200) will be happy to put you up for the night.

Katoomba is the largest town (population 9,000) but the real reason to visit is its proximity to the natural attractions. Nearby are the famous Three Sisters at Echo Point, which overlooks the dense forests of the Jamison Valley. The three pillar-like rocks take their name from an Aboriginal legend about sisters who were turned to stone by a witchdoctor in a bid to stop them marrying men from a forbidden tribe.

The Central Coast & Newcastle

A one-hour drive north of Sydney, the Central Coast has spectacular beaches, a lively surf culture and gorgeous national parks. Gosford is the largest town but, other than essential shopping facilities, has little to offer. The bustling seaside town of Terrigal is the best place to base yourself as it has lots of accommodation options and good places to eat. Everything is centred around the busy 4km beach, lined by tall Norfolk Pines. The Cove cafe at the eastern end of the beach has beautiful ocean views and good coffee. Both The Reef restaurant (www.reefrestaurant.com.au) and The Cowrie (www.thecowrie.com.au) have fabulous water views and award-winning cuisine (mains $30-$40). The best takeaway option is The Snapper Spot for beer-battered fish n' chips (02

4384 3780) or Hungry Wolf's Pizza & Pasta (02 4385 6555), both on the main street across from the beach. The Crowne Plaza (02 4907 5000) at the eastern end of the main strip has a huge outdoor beer garden and often has live entertainment.

Wollongong & Illawarra

Illawarra is an Aboriginal word meaning 'high and pleasant place by the sea', which pretty much rings true. Starting from Sydney's southern end and running all the way to Kiama, the 85km scenic stretch of coast boasts idyllic beaches, tranquil lakes and a string of national parks. The Sea Cliff Bridge, completed in 2005, is the most scenic route south, winding its way along the limestone cliffs with glorious views out to the Pacific Ocean. The best panorama by a long shot is on Bald Hill, a popular hang gliding spot. From here, follow the Grand Pacific Drive along the glittering ocean vista and lush forest to Bulli (the grand old Heritage Hotel is a cool spot for a beer in summer, 02 4284 5884, www.heritagehotel.com.au) and on to Wollongong. If you're into steam trains, check out the Illawarra Light Rail Museum at Albion Park (02 4256 4627).

Kangaroo Valley

Nestled between the South Coast and Southern Highlands, and just 159km south of Sydney, this tiny hamlet is surrounded by dairy farms, dense rainforest and a pretty river. Bird watching is big, as is bushwalking (there are more than 25 walking tracks in the valley) but watch out for snakes in spring and summer. Camping is popular (the Kangaroo Valley Tourist Park is right by the river, near the bridge, 1300

559 977) and the more adventurous will love horse riding up the mountain for fabulous views of the Shoalhaven Gorge (www.kangaroovalleyhorseriding.com), mountain biking (www.kangaroovalleyescapes.com.au) or canoeing down the Kangaroo River (www.kangaroovalleycanoes.com.au). If you're not much of a camper, Tall Trees B&B (02 4465 1208) and Clerevale (02 4465 1621) are good places to stay.

Driving through the lush scenery is a pleasure in itself. The narrow and winding Kangaroo Valley Road runs along steep sandstone escarpments but it's far more picturesque than the Princes Highway. You'll get good views across to Cambewarra Mountain from a lookout near Nowra.

Southern Highlands

First settled in the 1820s, when farmers discovered the fertile grazing land, this heritage-rich rural area became a desired address for the elite from the 1880s. It still retains its original aristocratic atmosphere with countless English-style estates, young boutique wineries (there are 15 open cellar doors) and award-winning restaurants. Don't miss the area's new five-star winery, Centennial Vineyards, with an excellent country-style restaurant attached (02 4861 8700, www.centennial.net.au). If you plan to stop overnight, Berrima Guesthouse (02 4877 2277) and Peppers Manor House (02 4860 3111) both offer a comfortable place to lay your head. Three kilometres north of Berrima is the massive Berkelouw Book Barn (www.berkelouw.com.au), with a collection of rare, second hand books and a tranquil cafe.

Exploring

Further Out

Exploring

Tours & Sightseeing

A guided tour can be the best way to get your bearings in a new city. From Sydney by seaplane to treks through bushland and wine tasting in Hunter Valley, there really is something for everyone.

Activity Tours

Getabout 4WD Adventure Tours
02 8822 5656
32 Witney St, Prospect, Outer West
www.getabout.net

Most 4WD day tours don't really go that far into the bush but you do get to traverse more picturesque (and bumpier) roads than on a tour bus. Smaller groups also mean you have more flexibility in the day's itinerary. This firm also offers a guided nighttime spotlight tour so you can see some of Australia's bush creatures, such as kangaroos, possums, wombats and owls, which are livelier after dark. Day tours are from $225 including lunch and snacks. 🚉 Central Station and 🚌 700

Sydney Tour Skywalk
02 9333 9222
100 Market St, Central
www.skywalk.com.au

Adrenalin junkies might not feel an almighty rush, but seeing Sydney from the outdoor platform is still more exciting than surveying the skyline from behind glass. Only open since 2005, the views from up here are spectacular, and at 260m it's almost double the height of the Harbour Bridge. If you feel queasy, try not to chunder over the safety ledge as you'll be fined $5,000. You're harnessed to safety railings the whole time and the guides let you in on interesting city secrets – like the snipers allegedly stationed on the balcony of the US Embassy since September 2001. Admission includes access to the Observation Deck and OzTrek, a goofy simulated ride through Australia on 180 degree screens. Open from 09:00-00:15. Adult $109, child $85 (must be 10 years or older).

Circular Quay, Map p.234 A3 **23**

Bonza Bike Tours
02 9331 1127
Various locations
www.bonzabiketours.com

Although not an overly bike-friendly city, these tours will have you easily dodging Sydney traffic. You'll cover a larger area including spots other tours miss, like the Walsh Bay wharves, with a welcome pit stop at the charming The Hero of Waterloo pub. Riding through the various parks is enjoyable but the biggest thrill is the 'car park run', a dizzying but exhilarating hurtle down the spiralling five-floor car park under the Opera House. There are regular stops so even the less fit won't find it too tough. Choose between a two-hour Sydney highlights tour ($70, departs 14:00), or the Sydney classic tour (three and a half hours, $70, departs 10:30). Tours to the less touristy north side are also available.

Sydney Harbour Kayak
02 9960 4389
Spit Bridge, Mosman
www.sydneyharbourkayaks.com

After a brief introduction and run down on safety and kayaking techniques, it's time to get up close and personal to harbour life. Choose from several different routes, including the main harbour taking in the bridge and Opera House to the more remote that take you into the bays and beaches of Middle Harbour. Morning tea is provided on a secluded beach. Tours cost $99 and depart from Spit Road, The Spit Bridge, Mosman. North Sydney and 480 Map p.225 D1

Boat Tours

Captain Cook Cruises   02 9206 1100
Various locations, Darling Harbour   www.captaincook.com.au
Catamarans leave roughly every half hour and tours range from basic sightseeing to dinner cruises. They also have a weekend-long cruise; after dinner on Friday night the ship docks near the Opera House before drifting up and down the harbour and Parramatta River (you are dropped off to stretch your legs during the day at famous landmarks). The cabins are small but there's plenty of space on the top deck to enjoy the harbour sites. Leaves Friday at 18:00, returns Sunday at 15:00. From $420 per person twin share, all meals included. Basic sightseeing cruise: adult $24, child $20, concession $12, family $59. Darling Park

Magistic Cruises   02 8296 7222
King St Wharf, Darling Harbour   www.magisticcruises.com.au
These catamarans are the newest on the harbour. The massive windows ensure great views from inside but you can also go on one of the decks to take scenic shots. Basic sightseeing cruises include one free beer. The freshly cooked buffet

lunch or dinner cruises have delicious king prawns, oysters and a good selection of hot main meals plus cake, cheese and crackers (alcohol is extra). Table service for drinks is fast and efficient. Thankfully the pre-recorded GPS commentary is much more low-key than traditional live commentary. Mondays and Tuesdays are generally quieter. Boats leave from King Street Wharf and Circular Quay. Adult $25, child $18.50, family $69 for one hour basic sightseeing tour. Lunch cruise: $66. Dinner cruise: $89. Darling Park, Map p.231 E2 **30**

Manly Ferry
Circular Quay

13 1500
www.sydneyferries.info

This is the locals' cruise of choice. The half-hour trip from Circular Quay to Manly is by far the best value-for-money cruise. There's no commentary, which some might find a blessing, and you can spend a few hours exploring Manly at the other end. In peak summer periods it can be a bit of a squash, but it's designed to be public transport, rather than a tour. Adult $6.20, child $3.10. Circular Quay, Map p.227 D4 **31**

Bus Tours

City Sightseeing
Various locations

02 9567 8400
www.city-sightseeing.com

This is the same outfit that runs double decker bus tours in Europe and you'll have to scramble for seats on the open top deck (don't forget a hat and sunnies or you'll fry). This bus offers two routes with a pre-recorded English commentary. The Sydney tour runs from Darling Harbour, through the CBD and Kings Cross, and ends at Circular Quay, while the eastern suburbs tour leaves from Central station and goes to Bondi and Double Bay via Paddington. Tickets are valid for both routes for 24 hours from the time of purchase. You can buy them on board or at The Rocks and Darling Harbour Visitor Centres. Adult $30, child $15, concession $25, family $75.

Sydney Explorer
Various locations
13 1500
www.sydneypass.info

You can hop on and off this route as you please. The buses wind their way through the city's central sights from Circular Quay east to Kings Cross, south to Surry Hills, west to Darling Harbour and across the bridge to Luna Park. Commentary is provided and tickets are available onboard. Adult $39, child $19, family $97. Every 20 minutes from 08:40-17:20.

Helicopter & Plane Tours

Blue Sky Helicopters
Ross Smith Ave, Sydney Airport
02 9700 7888
www.blueskyhelicopters.com

Try spotting a migrating whale from the sky. Even if you don't see any, the city looks incredible. If you can afford the hefty price, it's worth considering. It's $525 for 60 minutes and runs in June, July, September and November only. Domestic Airport

Sydney By Seaplane
Seaplane Base, Lyne Park
1300 656 787
www.sydneybyseaplane.com

This tour is about as Hollywood as it gets. Based next to Sydney's swanky Catalina restaurant, (02 9371 0555), you can

choose between five different scenic flights over the harbour and beaches; these include lunch at various swish spots on the northern beaches ($320-$460 per person).
Bondi Junction and 387

Sydney Helitours 02 9317 3402
472 Ross Smith Ave www.sydneyhelitours.com.au
You'll need a strong stomach for the twists and turns on the Thrill Seekers Flight ($199 per person for 20 minutes), and be warned, the choppers are doorless so it's not for the fainthearted. Scenic flights over the harbour, beaches and to the Blue Mountains are also available in regular helicopters (20-90 minutes, from $189 to $675). Domestic Airport

Walking Tours

Aboriginal Heritage Tour 02 9231 8134
Moore Room, Royal Botanic Gdns www.rbgsyd.nsw.gov.au
This one-hour tour shows the Royal Botanic Gardens from an Aboriginal perspective. Led by an Aborigine guide, you'll learn about the Cadigal people, the original indigenous inhabitants of this area, get to taste some bush foods and be treated to a traditional dance performance. Tours cost $20 and depart on Fridays at 14:00. Circular Quay and 399, Map p.234 C2 32

Blue Mountains Walkabout 0408 443 822
Faulconbridge Station www.bluemountainswalkabout.com
This tour takes you off the tourist track and aims to teach you about traditional Aboriginal life and Dreamtime stories

while you wander through the wilderness. Run by Aboriginal guide Evan Yanna Muru, the 8km trek will take you past ceremonial sites and ancient art and offers bush-tucker tastings. Take water, your own lunch and swimming gear. Moderate fitness is required and be prepared for slippery sections and rock scrambling. The walk begins at 10:00, leaving from Faulconbridge Railway Station platform. Tours are $95 per person. Faulconbridge Station

Bounce Walking Tours

1300 665 365
Wharf 6, Circular Quay   www.bouncewalkingtours.com

As well as tales of debauchery, plague and drunken sailors in The Rocks, Bounce do a tour through Kings Cross and the stories of sex, murder, corruption and violence give a good insight into Sydney's most notorious suburb. You'll meet in Circular Quay and catch a public bus to Kings Cross (included in the price). They also do a tour specifically for mums with prams. Depart Wharf 6, Circular Quay. Tickets are $25-$40.
 Circular Quay, Map p.226 C4 **33**

Sydney Architecture Walks

02 8239 2211
Various locations   www.sydneyarchitecture.org

As well as details on architectural styles, you'll learn about the history, politics and personal trivia that has made the cityscape what it is today. Wear sunglasses as you'll be staring skyward alot. Wednesday and Saturday, 10:30. Adult $25, concession $20 (includes entry to Museum of Sydney).

The Rocks Walking Tours   02 9247 6678
23 Playfair St, The Rocks   www.rockswalkingtours.com.au

The Rocks is one of the most historically important areas of Sydney. It's worth exploring the hidden alleys and cobbled courtyards on your own, but this tour gives a good insight into what life was like before the tourist shops. Tours depart Monday to Friday at 10:30, 12:30, 14:30 and Saturday to Sunday at 11:30 and 14:00. Adult $20, child $10.50, YHA member $16, family $50.50.   Circular Quay, Map p.226 C2 34

Wine Tours

Boutique Wine Tours   02 9499 5444
Hunter Valley   www.visitours.com.au

This is a great way to see the area and learn about wine. Knowledgeable guides lead you to some fabulous boutique wineries, many of which are family-run and stick to traditional methods, like storing in oak barrels (rather than tossing oak chips into the juice) to produce an authentic flavour. The all-inclusive tour for $99 is the best value and includes lunch. The gourmet option costs $139.   Maitland Station

Hunter Valley Wine and Dine Carriages   0410 515 358
Hunter Valley   www.huntervalleycarriages.com.au

This is a fun way to get some fresh air at a slow and steady country pace. Horse-drawn carriages take up to 10 people to five small wineries over a full day for $85 with a restaurant lunch, $75 with an organised picnic.   Maitland Station

Sports & Spas

110 Activities
118 Spectator Sports
122 Spas & Massage Centres

Sports & Spas

Activities

From golf to surfing and checking out the quirky marine life in its oceans, Sydney's got a wealth of activities to keep the boredom at bay.

Wherever you go in Sydney, you'll see people enjoying a city that lends itself perfectly to outdoor pursuits. With warm summers and temperate winters, the clear waters and gorgeous beaches of Sydney's harbour and coastline are a focal point for many visitors. You can take to the waves on a surfboard or enjoy an afternoon sailing, diving or snorkelling. Or, try one of the city's swimming baths for a refreshing dip or a challenging few hours golfing on some of its finest greens.

Facilities at the city's public sports centres often comprise multipurpose indoor courts for basketball, netball, volleyball or badminton, as well as a swimming pool and tennis courts. Designed to be used by anyone and everyone, these centres usually operate on a drop-in basis and fees are generally between $10 and $15 per visit, perfect for keeping you active during your stay.

On the other hand, if you need some serious pampering, polishing and R&R, there's an abundant selection of luxurious health spas and dedicated massage centres dotted about the place. Whatever you choose to do, one thing is for certain - this is one city where you'll never be stuck for something to do.

Diving

Abyss Scuba Diving
02 9583 9662
278 Rocky Point Rd, Ramsgate   www.abyss.com.au

Abyss offer regular PADI certificate courses for $445, with discounts for group bookings. They also offer a range of more advanced courses, a refresher course, and regular excursions, one of which includes a three-day, cage-diving trip in waters frequented by Great White sharks. Kogarah and 477/476

Dive Centre Manly
02 9977 4355
10 Belgrave St, Manly   www.divesydney.com

This PADI certified training centre offers a range of full and part-time courses. They also have multilingual instructors available. Their mid-week, four-day learn-to-dive programme costs $395 and covers theory, pool training, four ocean dives and equipment rental. Map p.242 B2

Oceanworld
02 8251 7877
West Esplanade, Manly   www.sharkdive.oceanworld.com.au

Whether you're a novice or an experienced diver, you can visit the huge aquarium at Manly for the chance to get up close and personal with some of its inhabitants. Choose from a range of 30 minute dives that will bring you face to face with huge grey nurse and wobbegong sharks, moray eels, stingrays, sea turtles and other marine life. Prices range from $180 to $245. Participants must be 14 years or over and bookings are essential. Map p.242 A2

Snorkel Inn
49 President Ave, Kogarah

02 9588 5042
www.snorkelinn.com.au

Snorkel Inn run their dive school from south of Sydney, in Kogarah, and offer learn-to-dive scuba programmes from $365 per person. They also run specialist courses in wreck or night diving and underwater photography. If you've caught the diving bug after a few dips and want to buy your own gear, they also often sell old dive school equipment for reasonable prices. Kogarah

Golf

Bondi Golf Course
5 Military Rd, Bondi

02 9130 3170
www.bondigolf.com.au

This is a challenging, nine-hole, old-style course designed to help you work on your short game. Recently landscaped with a new green, it's also a historical landmark complete with Aboriginal stone carvings. You can also do whale-watching here as you practice your swing. The fee for nine holes is $15, golf lessons are $50 and set hire is $18.50. Booking is essential.
Bondi Junction and 380/389, Map p.225 E4

Moore Park Golf Course
Anzac Pde, Moore Park

02 9663 1064
www.mooreparkgolf.com.au

This grade one club is just 10 minutes from Sydney's CBD. It has 18 holes, large greens, rolling fairways and views across the city. It's suitable for all abilities and also contains a driving range, two bars, a bistro and function rooms. Weekend fees are $50 for a round. 392/397/399, Map p.225 D4

Kayaking

Sydney Harbour Kayak 02 9960 4389
Spit Rd, Mosman www.sydneyharbourkayaks.com
While the cruises might be faster, kayaking allows you to get up close to harbour life. There are several different routes, from the obvious (into the main harbour with views of the bridge and Opera House), to the more remote (taking you into the bays and beaches of Middle Harbour). A generous morning tea is provided during a stop at a secluded beach where you'll feel a million miles from the city. Tours cost $99 (including the morning tea) and depart from Spit Road, Mosman.

North Sydney and 230/228, Map p.225 D1

Sailing

Aquablue 02 9981 4393
Level 1, 3 Brady St, Mosman www.aquabluecharters.com.au
Aquablue offers an impressive selection of vessels. Their fleet includes luxury cruisers, yachts and catamarans and tall ships. They're also specialists in providing interactive entertainment, from an onboard casino to a laser shooting experience.

North Sydney and 230/228, Map p.225 D2

Ausail 02 9960 5451
Various locations www.ausail.com.au
Recognised by Yachting Australia, Ausail's courses are taught aboard luxury Catalina yachts by friendly, patient instructors. An introductory course for absolute beginners costs

$440. Other courses cover skipper training, sailing theory, navigation, weather interpretation and more.

EastSail
02 9327 1166
D'Albora Marinas, Rushcutters Bay   www.eastsail.com.au
EastSail offer charter bareboat yachts (for experienced sailors) or boats with skippers (an additional $55 per hour). Their largest yacht can sleep up to 20. Boats can be taken for between four hours and two days. Kings Cross, Map p.225 D3

Quayside Charters
02 9341 8226
Various locations   www.quaysidecharters.com.au
Specialising in luxury and special event charters, Quayside caters for groups from two to 650 people, with all kinds of vessels available for harbour weddings, whale watching events, New Year celebrations and fishing expeditions. They can also supply fine dining menus, DJs, fireworks and hired entertainers.

Sail Australia
1800 606 111
Various locations   www.sailaustralia.com.au
Sail Australia has chartered yachts and cruisers, either bareboat or skippered, for special events, parties and sports fishing. You can also combine pampering treats with your day on the waves, such as a full body massage.

Simply Sailing
02 9451 2511
Clontarf, North Sydney   www.simplysailing.com.au
You can choose from bareboat and skippered vessels, ranging from 35 to 42 foot. The company can organise everything

Activities **Sports & Spas**

and they have an overnight anchorage option; the crew drop anchor, and you are left to an overnight stay on Sydney Harbour. North Sydney and 230/228, Map p.225 E2

Surfing

Let's Go Surfing 02 9365 1800
128 Ramsgate Ave, Bondi

Bondi's only licensed surf school runs a Bondi Surf Experience beginner's course, which teaches you how to safely get up on your board and out on a wave. Classes are limited to six or less and the cost is $59 (low season) or $69 (high season) for the two-hour session. All gear is provided. Map p.239 F1

Manly Surf School 02 9977 6977
Manly Beach, Opp Pine St www.manlysurfschool.com

This school runs daily lessons from Manly and other beaches around Sydney. Safe, stable surfboards and wetsuits are provided and beginners lessons cover how to ride, surf safety and surf awareness. Tuition costs $55 for one lesson. Private one-on-one tuition costs $80 an hour. Map p.242 C1

Waves Surf School 1800 851 101
Various locations www.wavessurfschool.com.au

Waves Surf School offer one-day surf trips to the Royal National Park south of Sydney for $75, which includes two surf lessons, all equipment, lunch, transfers and a 4WD on the beach and sand dunes. They guarantee that you'll be riding a wave by the end of the day. Pick up from various locations.

Swimming Baths

Bondi Icebergs Club 02 9130 3120
Southern end of Bondi Beach www.icebergs.com.au

This open-air venue is part rock pool, thanks to the ocean waves that crash over its edge. Open daily except Thursdays. Adult entry fee is $4.50. Map p.239 E3

McIvers Baths
Beach St, Coogee

This secluded pool is the last remaining ladies-only seawater pool in Australia. It boasts spectacular views and is pretty well screened from the surrounding area. Amenities and changing rooms are on site. Open 12:00-17:00. Bondi Junction and 314

North Sydney Olympic Pool 02 9955 2309
Milsons Point, North Sydney

Set at the edge of the harbour, this complex houses an Olympic sized open-air pool and a 25-metre indoor pool with sauna, spa and cafe. Adult $5.10, child $2.50, sauna/spa $6.30. Open Monday to Friday 05:30-21:00; Saturday to Sunday 07:00-19:00. Wheelchair access. Map p.240 A4

Wylie's Baths 02 9665 2838
Neptune St, Coogee

This Edwardian-era pool built into the rocks just south of Coogee beach is a treat. Surrounded by a raised boardwalk, and complete with a little cafe, it's also the perfect spot for sunbathing. Entry is $3 per adult. Bondi Junction and 314

Sports & Spas / Activities

Spectator Sports

Catch a game or indulge in a flutter on the horses; supporting the local hotshots is all good, adrenalin packed, sporting fun.

If you love sport then Sydney is your dream city. Most spectator sports are played here to the very highest level. For the main venues, head to Moore Park where you'll find the magnificent Sydney Cricket Ground (SCG) and the Aussie Stadium next door, which hosts rugby league, union and soccer matches. Down the road is Randwick Racecourse where the big horse races take place, and out at Sydney Olympic Park is Stadium Australia, now known as Telstra Stadium because of its sponsor. Also on the complex is the aquatic centre, where big swim meets are held.

Aussie Rules

Australian Rules Football began in Melbourne as a winter exercise for cricketers, which is why it's played on an oval pitch. It's similar to Gaelic Football but there are no direct links.

Sports Venues

Acer Arena	Homebush	02 8765 4321
Aussie Stadium	Moore Park	02 9360 6601
Randwick Racecourse	Alison Road	02 9663 8400
Sydney Cricket Ground	Moore Park	02 9360 6601
Telstra Stadium	Homebush	02 8765 2000

This is the most family-oriented winter sport. It is played from March to August in a series of matches with teams from around the country, leading up the Grand Final, which is played at the Melbourne Cricket Ground (MCG) in September every year.

The Swans are the only Sydney AFL team and wear distinctive red and white stripes. Their home base is the Sydney Cricket Ground (SCG) at Moore Park, but they also play some matches at Telstra Stadium (see table opposite). For more information on the sport, visit www.afl.com.au.

Cricket

The country pours money and serious energy into training and nurturing cricketing talent; no surprise then that the national team are the undisputed world champions.

Cricket is played from October to March and domestic competitions are run on a state-by-state basis, as well as local intra-state levels. The world famous Sydney Cricket Ground or SCG (www.cricketnsw.com.au) is home to the New South Wales team (the Blues) and the first recorded match was played there in 1854.

You'll never have a problem keeping score; cricket is sporting religion here with TV, radio and newspapers following matches ball by ball. For more information on the sport, see www.cricket.com.au.

Rugby League

Rugby league is a hard, physical game born in the poor northern towns of England but is now more popular in

Australia than in its country of origin. There is a continuing tussle between league and its rival, rugby union, for players and support. A number of players have switched between the two codes. While league is viewed as working class, union is considered more the domain of middle class professionals. It's the closest Australia gets to a class war.

Some 16 clubs battle it out through the winter season, leading up to a Grand Final in early October, which is always held at the Telstra Stadium and can draw 100,000 spectators.

There are eight teams to support (half the national competition): Roosters in the eastern suburbs, Rabbitohs in south Sydney, Manly Sea Eagles, Eels in Parramatta, Panthers in Penrith, Sharks in Cronulla, Wests Tigers in Concord, or Bulldogs in south-west Sydney. For more see www.nrl.com.

State of Origin
Hyped as rugby league's toughest battle, this three-match series pits the two biggest league-playing states, New South Wales ('Blues') and Queensland ('Maroons'), against each other. Players turn out for the state where they first played professionally, so club team-mates are often on opposing sides. The games are ferociously competitive and normally very close.

Rugby Union
Union is seen as a family spectator sport with virtually no history of crowd violence, but big attendances are reserved for international matches. The Sydney team, which is really a team for the whole of New South

Wales is called the Waratahs (named after a flower found in the state). They're based at Aussie Stadium. The Waratahs play as part of a Super 14 competition involving 13 other teams from Australia, New Zealand and South Africa. For more general information on the sport, try www.rugby.com.au.

Soccer

Historically soccer has been unpopular, because Aussie rules and rugby dominate the winter season. A switch to a summer season (August-February) means it is now the city's fastest developing sport. It is known as soccer rather than football to avoid confusion with the aforementioned sports (all known colloquially as footie). The national A League includes seven teams (with one from New Zealand). Sydneysiders cheer for Sydney FC (www.sydneyfc.com), who play at Aussie Stadium. For more, visit Football Federation Australia (www.footballaustralia.com.au) or the A League (www.a-league.com.au).

Horse Racing

Racing in Australia has always been popular, possibly because it is so closely aligned with betting; Australians are second only to the Japanese in their passion for a flutter. If you're a fan of horseracing, make your way to Royal Randwick. This historic racecourse is home to the Australian Jockey Club (9663 8400, www.ajc.org.au) which holds regular race days throughout the year, offering a great day out and an opportunity to dress up. Sydney's other course, Warwick Farm (9602 6199), in the city's south-west also holds regular race meets.

Spas & Massage Centres

Splash out, indulge and luxuriate in the city's finest spas and massage centres. After all, it wouldn't be a holiday without some serious pampering.

There's no shortage of spas in Sydney, all promising to bring you back to good health. While specific treatments vary from one place to the next, most spas focus on key services like massage, exfoliation and facials and more unusual treatments. Standards vary but generally, the plusher the spa, the better the service, so go on and splurge for a really luxurious treat.

Aveda Concept Salon & Spa
QVB, 455 George St, CBD
02 8198 8203
www.aveda.com

Well known for their skincare and beauty products, Aveda's concept salon is also one of Sydney's top spas. Try one of their signature treatments, like the deluxe Himalayan Rejuvenation treatment, which is two hours of Ayurvedic purification, incorporating an aromatic steam inhalation, exfoliation and friction massage, a special steam canopy and then a continuous stream of warm plant oil over the 'third eye'. It's a strange but deeply soothing sensation. Before your treatment starts you'll receive a complimentary Aveda herbal tea. You will be asked to complete a quick questionnaire as you enjoy your tea so that you can receive a tailored consultation based on your skin type, using products specifically suited to your skin's needs. Map p.231 F3 [11]

Observatory Spa, p.124

The Last Resort

02 9300 6033
2 Brighton Blvd, Bondi www.lastresortwellbeing.com.au

Where possible, this beachside day spa uses organically grown products derived from native plants, fruits, desert salts and marine life. Their health lounge is a good spot to relax before and after your treatment. Here you'll be offered therapeutic teas before your pampering begins. You'll also be given a full lifestyle consultation before treatments, which include therapeutic massages, wraps and facials, as well as natural therapies like colonic hydrotherapy, homeopathy, reiki and clairvoyant readings. Bondi Junction and 389, Map p.225 E4

Sports & Spas

Millk Studio 02 8354 0318
177 Oxford St, Darlinghurst

This unisex spa is about as hi-tech as they come. Millk is the only Sydney salon to offer the NeoQi Cocoon Spa – a full size space age capsule with built-in infra-red and steam sauna, chromatherapy (light therapy), and both hydro and air bubble massage. Their Square Pulse hair removal treatments are some of the best currently on the market. The range of treatments is impressive and the spa provides quite a personalised experience. Map p.236 B2 **10**

Observatory Hotel Day Spa 02 9256 2222
89-113 Kent St, CBD www.observatoryhotel.com.au

Set in one of Sydney's most prestigious hotels, this salon pampers stressed out men and women. Products include Kodo massage (which is inspired by Aboriginal techniques), and Tibetan Bell treatment, which mixes massage and sound therapy. The spa also offers facials, body wraps, mud masks and more. They recommend you arrive early to make full use of their services, and guests who indulge in any one-hour treatment also receive free entry to their luxury pool, spa, steam room and sauna. Map p.226 off A4 **12**

Soul Day Spa 02 9389 5748
101 Oxford St, Darlinghurst www.souldayspa.com.au

With oriental style decor and a practical, no nonsense approach, this unassuming day spa offers Dermalogica-based treatments including massage, exfoliation and mud wraps. They cater to both men and women, and have a range of mother and daughter, birthday and hen party packages. Their full body Dead Sea salt exfoliation is particularly good for removing dry skin and encouraging circulation. After the ensuing moisturising body treatment, you'll emerge glowing from head to toe. Map p.236 B2 7

Spa Chakra
02 9369 0888
6 Cowper Wharf Rd, Woolloomooloo www.spachakra.com

Spa settings don't get much more impressive than this. It's set next to the water, in the five-star boutique Blue Hotel, in the trendy suburb of Woolloomooloo and has views across the harbour and the Botanic Gardens. The spa itself is spacious and elegant, with 12 treatment rooms and a relaxation lounge, as well as hydrotherapy and Vichy showers. If you're staying at the hotel itself, they offer an in-room service.
Map p.235 D3 8

Massage

The following places are distinct from those above because they offer massage only, rather than the therapies and treatments on offer at the spas.

Glebe Healing Centre
02 9566 1222
1 Booth St, Annandale www.glebehealing.com.au

Offers all kinds of healing, including Swedish, shiatsu, remedial and traditional Chinese massage. Different massages focus on reducing pain, stimulating blood circulation and aiding deep relaxation. The centre is affiliated with the Australian College of Traditional Medicine. Town Hall and 413, Map p.224 A4

Jobonga Massage & Natural Therapy   02 9221 0030
33 Bligh St, CBD   www.jobonga.com.au

In the heart of the city lies Jobonga, a warm and inviting centre decorated in burnt orange tones. You'll be able to choose from aromatherapy, sports, Swedish, lymphatic drainage, pregnancy and reflexology massage. Practitioners are fully accredited and trained, and health club rebates are available. Map p.229 D2 **13**

Massage By The Sea at Wylie's Baths   0412 738 483
Neptune St, Coogee   www.massagebythesea.com.au

This outdoors, resort-style massage centre runs from Wylie's Baths, an Edwardian-era bathing pool built into the rocks just south of Coogee beach. Stretch out on a massage table on the raised boardwalk above the pool and drift off to the soothing sounds of the ocean as your therapist works some magic.

Bondi Junction and   314 / 339

The Sydney Ka Huna Centre   02 9358 3777
76 Oxford St, Surry Hills   www.kahunacentre.com.au

Hawaiian-style Ka Huna or Lomi Lomi massage is a powerful style of bodywork that will have you virtually floating out of the door. You're greeted by soothing music, aromatherapy oils and bright, friendly therapists who work hard to make you feel welcome. This isn't a massage for the prudish, as you'll need to strip right off, but a strategically placed sarong saves your dignity. If you're suffering from stress or even just physical aches and pains, this is an uplifting and transformative experience. Map p.236 B2

Spas & Massage Centres

Sports & Spas

Sydney **mini** Explorer

Shopping

- **130** Shopping Sydney
- **132** Hotspots
- **136** Markets
- **138** Shopping Malls
- **142** Department Stores
- **144** Where To Go For...

Shopping

Shopping Sydney

Welcome to the shopping Mecca of Sydney. Wander the city's streets and vibrant localities, browse the markets' exotic wares or take to the malls for a no-nonesense, guilt-free spendfest.

Shopping is the perfect pastime for a city often accused (mostly by Melbournites) of being superficial, and many Sydneysiders consider it a serious leisure pursuit. There's an experience to suit every taste: wandering through the night markets in Chinatown, browsing Australian designer fashions, picking out a vintage clothing gem in Surry Hills, whiling away a rainy day in a Glebe bookshop or picking up a bargain case of fine wine straight from the cellar door.

If you love to shop, you'll love Sydney. You'll find everything from old second-hand stores and weekend markets with hidden treasures, to boutiques stocking the best of designer bling. From paintings to DIY, delis and department stores, this arty city is brimming with life and shops to cater to every taste.

Pitt Street Mall in the city is the nucleus of shopping in Sydney – here you can find department stores like Myer and David Jones and a whole network of malls, with enough shops to satisfy the most needy addict. More info is on page 139. The nearby Queen Victoria Building offers a classy shopping experience beneath high ceilings and ornately designed stained-glass windows.

The Rocks is a little touristy, but worth a look with its eclectic mix of markets, opal merchants, kitsch souvenir shops and international designers.

You won't save money by shopping in Sydney; most items like clothes, electrical goods and furniture cost the same as in the US and the UK, and international clothing and cosmetic brands may be more expensive. There are two major sales a year, in June and after Christmas, when you can find a few bargains, although many shops also run sales intermittently throughout the year. Shop attendants are quite relaxed and may not offer assistance unless asked.

While shopping in Sydney is not cheap, it is unique. Designer fashion, jewellery, art, vintage clothing, and beachwear all have a distinctive local flavour. Take a wander down Oxford Street to check out local designers like Sass and Bide, or Collette Dinnigan.

Most shops are open seven days, usually until at least 17:00, and some have late-night shopping on Thursdays.

GST

All goods and services, except fresh vegetables and some medical items, attract the 10% goods and services tax, or GST. This is already included in the displayed price. When leaving the country, you can be refunded the GST paid on any item worth over $300 bought in the 30 days before your departure. To claim your refund, bring the item(s) along with your tax receipt to the airport and go to the GST refund counter. For more information, visit www.customs.gov.au.

Shopping

Hotspots

Take to the streets and browse eclectic markets in Glebe, glorious boutiques in Darlinghurst and Leichhardt or get arty in Newtown and The Rocks.

Glebe Point Road, Glebe

Perhaps its proximity to Sydney University has meant Glebe Point Road is less about fashion and more about intellectual pursuits. There are bookshops galore, including Gleebooks, Sappho, Gleebooks Second-hand and the large Collins bookstore in nearby Broadway Shopping Centre, all open late most nights. It's also a good spot for music, with De Capo, which sells sheet music, Fish Records selling CDs, and X for second-hand CDs and records. It gets pretty busy on Saturdays thanks to the Glebe markets, but for the rest of the week there's quite a relaxed atmosphere.

Map p.232 A3 **1**

Hall Street & Beyond, Bondi

While it's best known for the beach, Bondi's shopping credentials are rapidly on the rise. Bondi is a newcomer to the serious shopping trade – only recently have a number of shops opened that cater to the discerning and increasingly wealthy locals in this once working-class suburb. Shops like One Teaspoon and Tuchuzy will please those looking for designer fashion, and anyone looking for bathers will like Mambo, Rip Curl and Bikini Island. There's also the bookshop

Gertrude and Alice, as well as several high street fashion shops and homeware shops. Map p.239 E2 **2**

King Street, Newtown

Walking down King Street in Newtown has a cosmopolitan, bohemian feel, although the shops are becoming increasingly trendy. It's a long road and you can buy anything from new and second-hand books, furniture, boutique fashion, shoes, homeware and much more. If you're looking for clothes, shops like Dangerfield, Quick Brown Fox and Elvis 4 Cleo sell a good range of boutique designs. You can also get books at Gould's, the Cornstalk Bookshop or Better Read Than Dead. If you're looking for something a little more unusual, Eastern Flair sells a whole range of imported Asian items like furniture, cushions, jewellery and home accessories. There are also a few locals selling poems and artworks by the side of the road. King Street has a relaxed, whatever-may-come kind of attitude, and it's also pleasant just to wander down the road with the sound of buskers playing in your wake. Map p.241 A3 **3**

Norton Street, Leichhardt

Norton Street was once a quiet suburban shopping strip until Norton Street Plaza and The Italian Forum opened up in 2000, and a host of other shops followed suit. There are designer fashion boutiques and shops selling Italian shoes. You can spend hours at Berkelouw bookshop browsing the new books downstairs or the second hand books and CDs upstairs. The Italian Forum (see p.141) also has a number of designer shops and eclectic merchants. Map p.224 A4

Oxford Street, Darlinghurst

Oxford Street was once the jewel in Sydney's shopping crown, but there's been a lot of hand-wringing about the state of the precinct recently – critics say business is on the wane. But the street running straight through Darlinghurst ('Darling-it-hurts' or just plain 'Darlo' to locals) still has plenty to offer. The focus is on upmarket fashion like Sass and Bide, as well as boutiques, vintage stores and art galleries among the trendy cafes and bars. Oxford Street is also the main street for the Gay and Lesbian Mardi Gras and while many have moved on, there is still a palpable gay and lesbian presence here.

Map p.236 B1 4

The Rocks

In the shadow of the Harbour Bridge and next to Circular Quay, the shop facades in The Rocks are in the original terrace-style, dating back to the first white settlers. The same place where you can now buy a designer handbag may once have been the site of some convict conflict or a house wracked by the plague 200 years ago. While it caters well to tourists, you won't find many tacky souvenir shops (although there are a couple) – most shops here are at the designer end of the market. You can buy Aboriginal art, photographic prints of Sydney and clothing and accessories with prints from Australian artist Ken Done. If you're not after souvenirs there are designer shops like Louis Vuitton, bookshops, and the art shop at the nearby Museum of Contemporary Art in Circular Quay. It sells a curious range of arty products. There are markets at weekends. Map p.226

Shopping

Hotspots

Sydney **mini** Explorer

Shopping — Markets

Take a wander around one of Sydney's bustling markets as you listen to live music and pick up cut-price bargains and unique gifts, sampling locally-made mouthwatering treats as you go.

Bondi Markets
Bondi Primary School, Campbell Parade
The Bondi markets epitomise Bondi: a bit crowded and full of young designers alongside old locals selling bric-a-brac. The markets sell clothes (new, local designer, vintage and second-hand), bags, sunglasses, jewellery, books, homeware and all kinds of eclectic items fashioned by carpenters, sculptors and photographers. International celebrities often zip through on whistle-stop tours of Australia, and plenty of local identities and wannabes also haunt the crowded pathways. Open on Sundays, from 10:00-16:00. Map p.239 F1

Glebe Markets
Glebe Primary School, Glebe Point Rd
You can usually hear the Glebe Markets before you see them, thanks to the live local music that plays there every weekend. The Glebe market is one of Sydney's best for fun and atmosphere. If you don't want to buy anything it's nice to simply browse the stalls selling jewellery, second-hand books, photo frames, handmade clothes and bags, sunglasses,

vintage items and unusual gifts (wind chimes made from forks, anyone?) If you need a break there are also food stalls that sell freshly made Turkish, Indian and Mexican food, and plenty of grassy spots to sit and watch the band. It gets particularly busy around midday. Map p.232 A3 **6**

Paddington Markets
395 Oxford St, Paddington

Fashion designers Collette Dinnigan and Nicole Zimmerman both started out selling their designs at the Paddington Markets, and it's still a great place to check out budding Australian designers and pick up bargain designer clothing. Young designers often start out here to raise their profile and to see what customers like. You can also get jewellery, hats, scarves, furniture, homeware and arts and crafts. Prices are a little more expensive than other markets. Open Saturdays, from 10:00-16:00. Map p.237 F4 **7**

Paddy's Market
Hay Street, Chinatown

Paddy's Market is an indoor market. Unlike other markets, many stallholders sell factory-produced goods imported from overseas rather than locally made items. There's a fresh fruit and vegetable section, as well as stalls that sell clothes, sunglasses, CDs, jewellery and souvenirs. The atmosphere is not as pleasant as other markets – it can feel dingy inside and is sometimes crowded, but you can save money by shopping here rather than the retail shops. Daily, 09:30-19:00.

Map p.233 E2 **8**

Shopping Malls

There's plenty to keep the cash registers ringing between Pitt Street, the QVB and The Italian Forum, not to mention the bargain outlet stores. Relax those purse strings and enjoy some city shopping.

Birkenhead Point
Roseby St, Drummoyne
02 9181 3922
www.birkenheadpoint.com.au

The edge of Sydney Harbour is a glittering location for an outlet mall, where major retailers offer discounted stock that is out-of-season or simply didn't sell. Australian designers Morrissey, Marcs, Alannah Hill and David Lawrence all have outlet stores here, as do fashion stores Cue, Witchery, French Connection, Jag, Mambo, Atelier and many more. Shops sell genuinely discounted items and you can pick up some real bargains. There's also a Spotlight store selling a huge range of textiles, art and craft materials; as well as shops that sell surfwear, lingerie and music. There's a supermarket, grocer and chemist on the ground floor. 500/501/506, Map p.224 A3

Broadway Shopping Centre
Opp Victoria Park, Glebe
02 9213 3333
www.broadway-centre.com.au

Broadway Shopping Centre is a relatively new mall recognisable by its two soaring clock towers. The atmosphere among the three levels is light and bright although the shops are mostly franchises you'll have seen elsewhere. Many inner-westies do their grocery shopping here thanks to two supermarkets, a grocer, a bakery, a bottle shop and two butchers, which are usually open til 19:00. There's also a range of clothes shops, a large Collins bookstore (good for settling in at the internal cafe), a food court, cinema, and a medical centre. Kmart is also here. Map p.232 B3 **12**

Pitt Street Mall
Martin Place, CBD

02 9286 0111
www.shopping-sydney.com.au

Pitt Street Mall in the CBD is an open walkway through one of Sydney's busiest shopping precincts. The area includes department stores Myer and David Jones, plus other malls walled together including Mid-City Centre, Centrepoint Arcade (at the base of the enormous Centrepoint Tower), Skygarden, Glasshouse, and The Strand Arcade. Basically, Pitt Street Mall is the central catwalk through a labyrinth of mini malls which all interlink. It can be very easy to get lost. Thankfully there are plenty of maps to help you orientate yourself. There is a huge range of shops but the focus is on personal items like clothes, shoes, accessories, beauty products, books, CDs and DVDs. Map p.234 A3 **2**

Queen Victoria Building
455 George St, CBD

02 9264 9209
www.qvb.com.au

With its lofty ceilings, ornate hand railings and patterned floors, the Queen Victoria Building (QVB) is an elegant shopping experience. The shops inside reflect the surroundings with sophisticated decor and higher prices. Brands like Calvin Klein and Polo Ralph Lauren mix with high street fashion and a good selection of arts and antiques shops.

The QVB extends underground and you can walk through to Myer, Pitt Street Mall and Town Hall Station. If you need any information, the concierge staff are very helpful (found on the ground floor and level two). They also run free, daily tours. For a little side excursion, visit the talking dog out front, found just behind the statue of Queen Victoria. Map p.231 F4 **13**

Westfield Bondi Junction 02 9947 8000
500 Oxford St, Bondi www.westfield.com

This is like a luminous maze with over 3,000 shops interwoven across two large buildings. It's huge, dazzling and a little overwhelming. Westfield Bondi is different to the other malls around Sydney because of its scale, but also because of more upmarket stores like Alannah Hill, Saba, Oroton and Morrissey. There are the usual high street fashion stores, as well as phone shops, electronics and games shops, food shops and supermarkets, a food court and cinema. Map p.238 off A2 **10**

DFO 02 9748 9800
Cnr Homebush Bay & Underwood Rd www.dfo.com.au

DFO, or the Direct Factory Outlet, houses a range of shops that sell excess stock and samples from fashion designers. It is in Homebush, about 20 minutes drive west of the city. Stores include Lisa Ho, FCUK, Jag, Morrissey, Charlie Brown, Witchery, Tommy Hilfiger and many more. You can pick up plenty of bargains, but DFO is a somewhat drab mall with few other facilities. Still, it's a small price to pay for picking up a designer gown at 75% off the retail price. 🚇 Homebush

The Italian Forum
Norton St, Leichhardt

02 9518 0077
www.italianforum.com.au

Norton Street has long been billed as Sydney's little Italy, and the Italian Forum cemented this reputation. Designed to mimic an Italian plaza, with apartments overlooking restaurants and shops, the Forum somehow managed to avoid being tacky and actually fulfils its brief. The feel is relaxed, and surprisingly Italian. The central piazza is filled with restaurants, and live music and festivals are occasionally held here. There are designer clothing shops as well as an interesting shop called The Merchant of Venice, which stocks a dazzling selection of handmade masquerade masks, wall hangings and other beautiful oddities. Petersham, Map p.224 A4

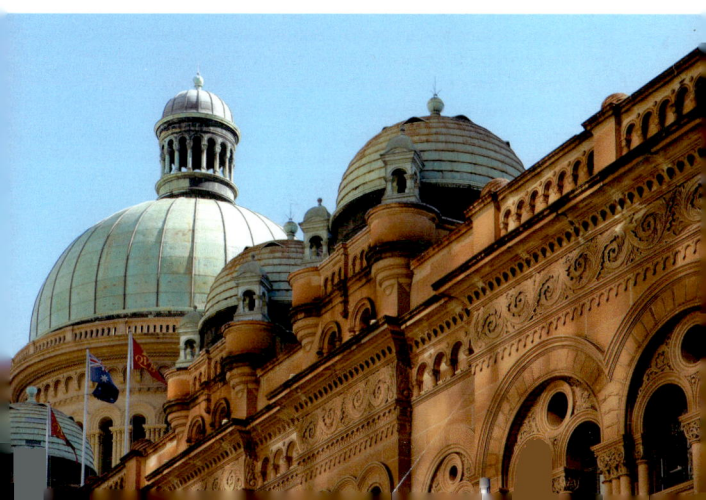

Shopping

Department Stores

From swanky, long-established department stores to modern shopping havens, Sydney's luxury shopping options won't disappoint.

David Jones
86 -108 Castlereagh St, CBD

02 9266 5544
www.davidjones.com.au

Once considered the shopping domain of snobbish grandmothers, David Jones has repositioned itself in the last five years for a much younger demographic. David Jones is slightly more upmarket than Myer and sells a wider choice of designer brands. You can buy a huge range of items including cosmetics and perfumes, hats and accessories, women's, men's and kids' fashions, homeware and furniture. David Jones in the city also has one of Sydney's best delicatessens. The impressive and massive food hall stocks all kinds of premium and obscure foods and beverages, including some fresh produce and bakery items, perfect for a picnic on a sunny afternoon. Map p.234 A2 **11**

Myer
436 George St, CBD

02 9238 9111
www.myer.com.au

Myer is Australia's most established department store, and has pride of place in the central shopping district of most big Australian cities, including Sydney. The first store was opened in Melbourne in 1900 by a poor Russian migrant named Sidney Myer and has been thriving ever since. The current store used to be called Grace Bros, but was bought out and renamed Myer a few years ago. The city Myer store has several floors, selling everything from cosmetics, shoes, fashion, accessories, homeware, furniture, books, music, DVDs, toys and games. Myer is especially renowned for its extensive cosmetics and perfume selection, and is also a good place to shop if you are looking for an outfit for the races – they have a great range of hats. Most products are brand names, so you'll be paying more but getting good quality. The store also sells prestige brands like Manolo Blahnik shoes or Estee Lauder cosmetics. Myer has two annual sales, one starting the day after Christmas and the other in mid-winter, although smaller sales occur throughout the year. Map p.231 F3 **14**

Peter's of Kensington   02 9662 1433
Anzac Pde, Kensington   www.petersofkensington.com.au

Peter's of Kensington, about 5kms south of the city, is a Sydney institution. It sells everything you could possibly want for your home – towels, linen, kitchenware, knives, lamps, ornaments, glassware, cutlery and cookware. From hammocks to clothes hangers, Peter's will have them every colour, shape and style. Peter's is a beautifully designed store, and it's a pleasure to wander through the aisles of glittering and lustrous new products. There are regular sales with genuine discounts and you can often save up to 50% off the marked price. There's also an internal cafe with a good selection of food available. 392/396/399

Shopping — Where To Go For...

Beachwear

You'll find everything you need all year round at department stores and surf shops located in beachside suburbs like Manly, Bondi and Coogee.

Most locals interpret beach fashion as a mix of high-street, market or vintage clothing worn over swimwear. Sunglasses and a large bag to carry your towel and book are a must; accessories like hats and market jewellery are also popular. For footwear stick to sandals or thongs (flip-flops), which are also allowed in most local pubs and cafes. Most local women wear bikinis or one-pieces. Most local men wear boardshorts (boardies) or speedos (referred to as 'budgie smugglers').

Local brands like Rip Curl (various locations, 02 9264 6777), Billabong and Mambo (17 Oxford St, 02 9331 8034) all make fashionable, good quality beachwear, priced from $50-$120. Women looking for innovative designs should also check out Seafolly and Tigerlily. These brands are available in most beachwear shops like Rip Curl and Bikini Island Swimwear (38 Campbell Parade, Bondi 02 9300 9446). One Teaspoon (86 Gould Street, 02 9365 1290) in Bondi is an (affordable) institution for beachside fashionistas and you'll find a good range of designer t-shirts, skirts and dresses retailing for under $90. Sue Rice (48 Ross Street, Glebe, 02 9660 0488) also specialises in custom made bathers in larger sizes for women, while Let's Go Surfing (128 Ramsgate Avenue, North Bondi, 02 9365 1800) sells beachwear as well as wetsuits, surfboards, and snorkel gear.

The Strand Arcade, off Pitt Street Mall (see p.139)

Where To Go For... **Shopping**

Aussie Designers

Sydney fashion is relaxed yet glamorous. Local designers Wheels & Doll Baby, Zimmerman and Charlie Brown have all made an international impact. David Jones stocks Australian designers but brands like Armani, Louis Vuitton and Dolce & Gabbana are also available in Sydney, with shops concentrated around The Rocks and in Double Bay. Sass & Bide at 132 Oxford Street (02 9360 3900) epitomises the Sydney women's look right now with its floaty tops and lacy skirts while Ksubi/Tsubi (02 8303 1400) at 82 Gould St in Bondi offers a range of relaxed-fit jeans and street wear for both men and women. For something a little special, Collette Dinnigan (33 William Street, Paddington, 02 9360 6691) is arguably Australia's leading designer and is famous for evening and bridal wear but also makes a wide range of skirts, jackets, tops, resort wear and eyewear.

Vintage Clothing

Vintage clothes are a big element of Sydney style. Surry Hills is the city's vintage hub, with Mr Stinky (482 Cleveland Street, 02 9310 7005) and C's Flashback (277 Crown Street, 02 9331 7833). Broadway Betty (259 Broadway, 02 9571 9422) is also nearby. Grandma Takes A Trip (263 Crown Street, 02 9356 3322) is perhaps Sydney's best-known vintage clothing shop and stocks a range of men's and women's vintage clothes and accessories including coats, suits, dresses, bags, sunglasses and jewellery and cufflinks. The Vintage Shop

(137 Castlereagh Street, 02 9267 7135) in the city is a treasure trove of clothing from a bygone era. Men's and Women's clothes are individually selected for their fabric, cut, and design and date from 1850 to 1980.

But, some shops are seriously over-priced. True vintage clothes are usually pre-1980 and selected for their fabric, cut, shape or distinctive design.

Books

Sydney has some wonderful bookshops that are destinations in their own right; the thriving local literature scene centres on many of the city's locally-owned bookshops which are well-stocked and have knowledgeable staff, and usually have an internal cafe.

Glebe is the city's best spot for book shopping, with Gleebooks (02 9660 2333, www.gleebooks.com.au) and Sappho Books (02 9552 4498, www.sapphobooks.com.au) next to each other at 49 and 51 Glebe Point Road and Collins in the Broadway Shopping Centre (p.138). The second-hand book stalls at the Saturday Glebe markets (p.136) can also turn up treats. Gleebooks is well-known and respected and stocks a large range of specialist books as well as international magazines. New books cost around $20-$40, but hardcover or specialty books may be more expensive. Berkelouw Books (02 9560 3200, www.berkelouw.com.au) has been in Sydney since 1812, and have shops in Leichhardt and Paddington. They sell a range of new books, stationery and designer notebooks, as well as a selection of second-hand books and CDs.

Shopping

Where To Go For...

Didgeridoos

If you want to learn to play the didgeridoo or 'didj', forget the straight painted pipes you find in souvenir shops. Authentic didgeridoos are produced in traditional communities and have an individual sound and an irregular shape. Aboriginal craftsmen carefully select part of a hardwood tree that has been hollowed out by termites, then cut and craft the instrument before finishing it with a rim of beeswax around the lip. Traditionally only played by men, mastering the didgeridoo (especially circular breathing) is tougher than it looks. Didj Beat Didjeridoo in The Rocks, (02 9251 4289, www.didjbeat.com) has a good range of authentic instruments and passionate staff who can give you playing tips.

Lingerie

Lacy, racy, patterned, pretty and practical, there's a bra available for every occasion in Sydney. Australia is home to a number of celebrity lingerie designers, most famously Elle McPherson (Elle McPherson Intimates) and Kylie Minogue (Love Kylie).

Elle McPherson Intimates includes an excellent collection of fashionable bras, briefs, g-strings, corsets and nightwear in well-fitting cuts while Love Kylie has more brazen designs.

Both Myer and David Jones (see p.142) have excellent selections of most major lingerie brands, including those mentioned above and Bendon, La Perla, Oroton, Calvin Klein and Loveable. If you're buying a gift, staff are very helpful at suggesting appealing designs and finding the right size.

Semi-precious Stones

You can buy jewellery everywhere in Sydney – in clothing shops, markets, department stores and from independent sellers. Beads or cheap materials made into jewellery are popular among locals but Australia is the world's number one opal manufacturer, and Sydney is a great place to buy these unique multicoloured gems. A&H Australian Opal House (02 9261 3193) and Australian Opal Market (413 Sussex Street, 02 92125671) are good places to buy genuine stones with a guarantee. You can get small, low-quality opals for $30, but a good stone can cost thousands.

Souvenirs

Sydney is not shy about flogging cheesy gifts to its hordes of tourists. You can go for fluffy kangaroos in the colours of the national rugby union team, wombat key rings, 'roo poo chocolate drops, proper ocker cork hats and almost anything else you can think of branded with the Aussie flag or bright gold and green. Much of this is to be found down by The Rocks (try Wombat At The Rocks, 27 Playfair Street, 02 9241 2632), and around Circular Quay. Aboriginal items are also to be found down here, such as didgeridoos and boomerangs, just be sure to check for their authenticity. Picolo Gifts (02 9262 6219) and Spring Row Gift Shop (02 9247 1851) both on George Street (333 and 115 respectively) are a good place to start. Otherwise, head to the Queen Victoria Building (p.139) and try Australian Geographic or Best of Australiana.

Going Out

- **152** Restaurants by Cuisine
- **154** Social Sydney
- **158** Bondi
- **162** CBD
- **170** Circular Quay & The Rocks
- **174** Darling Harbour & Chinatown
- **178** Kings Cross & Woolloomooloo
- **184** Manly
- **188** Newtown
- **192** North Sydney
- **194** Surry Hills & Darlinghurst
- **200** Entertainment

Going Out

OCEAN BEACH TEA ROOMS

ection

Restaurants by Cuisine

African	⭐ African Feeling	p.189
	Out of Africa	p.187
Australian	Aperitif	p.179
	Est	p.165
Chinese	⭐ Billy Kwong	p.195
	China Doll	p.180
	Kam Fook	p.160
	Manly Phoenix	p.185
Contemporary	Kirketon	p.197
	Ocean Room	p.173
	The Front	p.175
French	360 Bar and Dining	p.163
	Bilson's Restaurant	p.171
	⭐ glass brasserie	p.165
	⭐ Guillaume at Bennelong	p.172
	Industrie	p.166
Greek	Hellenic Club	p.166
	Kafenes	p.191
	Steki Taverna	p.191
Indian	Oh! Calcutta!	p.198
	Zaaffran	p.177
Italian	⭐ Hugo's Bar Pizza	p.181
	Will & Toby's	p.186
Japanese	Raw Bar	p.160
	⭐ Tetsuya's	p.168
	Yoshii	p.173

Restaurants by Cuisine

Korean	Haroo	p.193
Malaysian	Chinta Ria	p.175
	Malay Chinese	p.166
Mediterranean	Bambini Trust Café	p.163
	harbourkitchen&bar	p.172
	⭐ Icebergs Dining and Bar	p.159
	Manly Wharf Hotel	p.187
	Miltons	p.167
	Bondi Social	p.159
Mexican	Newton's Cucina	p.191
Middle Eastern	Arabella	p.189
	Café Mint	p.195
	Sumac	p.176
Seafood	Café Sydney	p.164
	Garfish	p.193
	Ice Cube	p.176
	Jellyfish	p.185
South American	Casapueblo	p.196
Spanish	⭐ Alhambra	p.185
	Grand Taverna	p.165
Steakhouse	Prime Restaurant	p.167
Thai	Arun Thai	p.179
	⭐ Nu's	p.193
Vegan	Green Gourmet	p.190
Vegetarian	Bodhi in the Park	p.163
	⭐ Govinda's	p.197
	Green Palace	p.190

Going Out

Sydney **mini** Explorer

Social Sydney

Going Out

Locals lead a hedonistic lifestyle. They love to eat, drink and socialise. This chapter tells you where and how.

In Sydney, there's something on every night of the week, whether it's the theatre, comedy or just having a laugh over a few schooners.

Sydney has two kinds of watering holes; down-to-earth pubs and swanky bars. The pubs are relaxed and convivial; the bars are showy and stylish.

Friday sees the suits knocking back Stellas in the CBD while Saturday night is when the clubbing and cocktail crowd come out to play. On the weekend, a night out starts at around 20:00 and if you're up for a big one, you can stumble on until dawn.

The city's nightlife options range from the operatic to the utterly camp, and its restaurant scene is the best in Australia.

Tipping

Tipping is not as common as in the US or Europe. Bar staff, waiting staff and taxi drivers get paid quite well and do not generally expect a tip, although any extra is always appreciated. In restaurants and cafes, the plusher the place the more a tip will be expected. Up to 10% is fine, but don't feel obliged if service is poor. If you can, leave cash, as credit card tips do not always reach the staff. Regular cafes and coffee shops may also have a tip pot on the counter.

Vegetarian

Sydney has a range of buzzing places to indulge in soy lattes and falafel burgers. Macro Wholefoods Café, see p.160, serves fresh, organic fare. Billy Kwong (p.195), was voted the 'best vegetarian restaurant' by The *Sydney Morning Herald Good Food Guide* in 2005. Another great place to go is Govindas (p.197), where a vegetarian buffet followed by a movie viewed on big, comfy couches will cost you less than $25. Glebe Point Road and Newtown are bursting with veggie options and you won't need to book. Most restaurants have more than one vegetarian option.

Gay & Lesbian

It's difficult to imagine a city with a more high profile gay scene than Sydney. Since the first, troubled gay rights marches of the 1970s, today's gay Sydney has become a vibrant, open and colourful community, with a scene focused around Oxford Street and the suburbs of Darlinghurst, Surry Hills and Newtown.

Gay culture has merged with the mainstream here. The main 'gay areas' have become the city's trendiest spots and gay and straight bars sit side by side. The

The Yellow Star
This natty yellow star is our way of highlighting places that we think merit extra praise. It could be the atmosphere, the food, the cocktails, the music or the crowd – but whatever the reason, any review that you see with the star attached is somewhere that we think is a bit special.

famed Gay and Lesbian Mardi Gras is a raucously camp highlight of Sydney's summer calendar.

Oxford Street is much more about mixed venues than exclusively gay hangouts. In Newtown, the scene is more grungy and diverse. It's also home to the Imperial (02 9519 9899), the bar made famous by the film *Priscilla, Queen of the Desert*, which still holds weekend drag shows. They try their level best to out-camp the film.

The age of consent is the same for both heterosexuals and homosexuals (16), and while there are occasional reports of gay-bashings and homophobia, particularly in some of the city's western suburbs, Sydney's residents are generally open and accepting. See also the Green Park Hotel on p.197 and Home on p.175. These are straight, but attract a gay crowd.

Fag Tag is worth a mention, though it isn't a bar or club. It's actually a group that takes over – or 'fag-tags' – non-gay venues around Sydney, organising parties and events for everyone on their mailing list. Their parties are well known and much loved and they always attract a wide following of what they proudly call 'gays, lesbians, friends, sisters, siblings, cousins, ex-fags, hags, can't-decides and closets'. Previous venues have included the famous Opera Bar of the Opera House, as well as all manner of other places around the city. Visit their website and join their mailing list for forthcoming event details; www.fagtag.com.au.

Drinking

Drinking is embedded in Aussie culture, and while there was a time when the country only exported weak lager, it is now known for its wines and premium beers.

Most restaurants have a licence – just make sure you bring your ID to show that you're over 18. The laws are strict and the fines hefty, so if you get caught drinking underage, expect to pay for it. Beer will cost you about $5, spirits $10 and soft drinks $4. Fruit cocktails are popular and it's common for people to ask for non-alcoholic mixes. The standard soft drinks are always available along with a variety of waters. Wine is very popular, because of the cheap, good quality produce Australia churns out. Even earthy, spit-and-sawdust pubs will have a decent drop on offer. One of Australia's best food magazines, *Gourmet Traveller*, regularly rates the best wines on offer. It's worth picking up a copy if you want to know the year's best bottles. Or, for a more detailed education, it may be worth taking a tour of vineyards outside the city. See p.107 for more.

Going Out: Bondi

The Bondi social scene is a mix of boozy backpackers, eastern suburb sophisticates and laid back surfers.

Campbell Parade, the main strip that runs behind Bondi's beach, has a string of eating and drinking options. Many of these are plain fast food spots selling burgers and fish and chips. Interspersed with souvenir and beachwear shops, it can give the feel of a typical seaside town anywhere in the English speaking world.

But, there are a number of gems tucked away and Bondi's social scene reflects those that live in the area. Backpackers and surfers gravitate here for the beach life and add a little colour and vitality to the bar scene.

Bondi is also popular for the trendy set and up towards Bondi Junction the leafy streets tend to appeal to young (fashionable) families.

Venue Finder

Kam Fook	Chinese	p.160
Raw Bar	Japanese	p.160
Icebergs Dining and Bar	Mediterranean	p.159
Bondi Social	Mediterranean	p.159
Gertrude & Alice	Cafe	p.159
Macro Wholefoods Café	Cafe	p.160

Bondi Social
Mediterranean
1st Floor, 38 Campbell Pde   02 9365 1788
The Bondi Social tries to mix inner city chic with the eastern suburbs vibe. It largely succeeds. The interior is all bare wooden floors and white tablecloths, and the narrow terrace over Campbell Parade has a view of the strutting throng below. The food is crisp Mediterranean. It does brunch from 08:30, and dinner from 17:00. Bondi Junction and 380, Map p.239 E3 **1**

Gertrude & Alice
Cafe
40 Hall St   02 9130 5155
With its cosy surroundings and second-hand books, it's easy to lose an afternoon to eating and reading, completely oblivious to the Bondi buzz just outside. Regulars will tell you not to pass up a helping of the flourless chocolate cake, washed down with a freshly brewed coffee, while the Mediterranean and Middle Eastern mainstays such as open sandwiches are also popular. Bondi Junction, Map p.239 E2 **2**

Icebergs Dining Room and Bar
Mediterranean
1 Notts Ave   02 9365 9099
Sydneysiders go to Icebergs as much for the celebrity spotting as they do for the Mediterranean fare and million-dollar views. If you dine in the evening, catch the sun setting over the ocean as you tuck into a serving of stingray, silverbeet, asparagus and shitake and wood ear mushrooms prepared by chef Robert Marchetti. While the valet parking adds to the distinctive experience, the wine list will have you considering your transport options. Bondi Junction and 380, Map p.239 E3 **3**

Kam Fook
Westfield Bondi Junction

Chinese
02 9386 9889

The yum cha (a type of oriental breakfast tapas) here has locals lining up as early as 11:00 to score a table. Take your pick from the yum cha trolleys that cruise the room or pick from the a la carte menu. The entertainment comes from traditionally-clad Chinese musicians. You can get your fill for around $20, with entrees starting at $6 and mains at $15.

Bondi Junction, Map p.238 off A2 **5**

Raw Bar
136 Wairoa Ave

Japanese
02 9365 7200

Food in this modern Japanese eatery is fresh and fast and comes complete with that Bondi vibe. Loyal diners, who flock here for generous servings, will tell you not to pass up the bento box with teriyaki chicken, sushi, sashimi, tempura and miso for around $24, but the prawn tempura rolls really do the trick. There are no reservations here; it's first come, first served. Bondi Junction, Map p.239 F1 **4**

Macro Wholefoods Café
31-37 Oxford St

Cafe
02 9004 1240

Fussy foodies love this place for its varied menu, which incorporates all tastes and tolerances, from gluten-free to soy. Don't leave without experiencing the buckwheat pancakes with berries and bananas or the scrambled tofu, washed down with a cup of dandelion tea.

Bondi Junction, Map p.238 off A2 **85**

Going Out

Bondi

Sydney **mini** Explorer

Going Out

CBD

The central business district has some of the city's finest dining options and funkiest bars and clubs.

The CBD may seem a little quiet once the nine to fivers have gone home for the day, but central Sydney has a bounty of fine bars, clubs and restaurants to be discovered.

Venue Finder

Est	Australian	p.165
360 Bar and Dining	French	p.163
glass brasserie	French	p.165
Industrie	French	p.166
Hellenic Club	Greek	p.166
Tetsuya's	Japanese	p.168
Malay Chinese	Malaysian	p.166
Bambini Trust Café	Mediterranean	p.163
Miltons	Mediterranean	p.167
Café Sydney	Seafood	p.164
Grand Taverna	Spanish	p.165
Prime Restaurant	Steakhouse	p.167
Bodhi in the Park	Vegetarian	p.163
Bristol Arms Retro Hotel	Nightclub	p.164
Chinese Laundry	Nightclub	p.164
Purple Sneakers	Nightclub	p.167
Tank	Nightclub	p.168
The Slip Inn	Pub	p.168

360 Bar and Dining

100 Market St

French
02 9235 2188

Book well in advance for a table at the southern hemisphere's highest restaurant. With a revolving floor that ensures a bird's-eye view of the city from every table, 360 is a unique experience. Add to this great food, a carefully selected winelist, relaxing dim lighting and dark, hand-carved mahogany surrounds and you're in for a real treat. St James, Map p.231 F3 **7**

Bambini Trust Café

185 Elizabeth St

Mediterranean
02 9283 7098

Everything is large at Bambini Trust Café, from the grand pillared entrance to the servings of pumpkin ravioli and ricotta. While dinner here isn't easily forgotten, those in the know also head to this immaculate city cafe to sample the breakfast menu. You could try the house bircher muesli with fresh fruits or the perfectly poached eggs with smoked salmon or ham, topped with spinach and creamy hollandaise.

Circular Quay, Map p.229 D4 **8**

Bodhi in the Park

College St, Cook and Phillip Park

Vegetarian
02 9360 2523

You can relax here all afternoon in the courtyard as you tuck into vegetarian yum cha or other Asian delights. Bodhi in the Park is a tranquil escape from the city buzz and the alfresco dining makes it perfect for a weekend catch up with friends. Yum cha ranges from $4.50 to $7.50. While service can be patchy and aloof at times, the menu makes up for it.

St James, Map p.234 B4 **86**

Bristol Arms Retro Hotel

81 Sussex St

Nightclub
02 9262 5491

It's not just the five floors and seven bars that bring the happy young things to Retro Nightclub. As its name suggests, the tunes here are reflective of eras past – from the 60s through to the 90s. Here, Michael Jackson is still cool and Madonna young. The huge dance floors quickly fill to the beats of the in-house DJs, making Retro one of city's most popular nightspots. In this place it doesn't matter if you don't do cool and the bus stop isn't anything to do with public transport. 🚇 Wynyard, Map p.231 E2 **10**

Café Sydney

31 Alfred St

Seafood
02 9251 8683

You'll be hard pressed to find a Sydneysider who hasn't at least heard of this spot and its spectacular harbour views. The dishes take their inspiration from Japan, Italy, India, Morocco and Thailand and the theme is ultimately seafood, to be enjoyed indoors or out on the sheltered terrace. The menu is extensive and includes a tempting seafood platter for $135. It gets busy with office workers during the day but is also popular for special occasions, and you can hire out a private dining room for 14. 🚇 Circular Quay, Map p.226 C4 **11**

Chinese Laundry

111 Sussex St

Nightclub
02 9240 3000

As the party gets started at the well-frequented Slip Inn upstairs, clubbers-in-the-know are warming up in the cool depths of Asian-inspired Chinese Laundry down below. The underground nightclub is a magnet for local and international DJs, as well as live musicians, who belt out their tunes to an appreciative, party-hard crowd. Fun-loving staff pour their liquor with passion and add to the overall friendly vibe of the place.   Wynyard, Map p.231 E2 **12**

Est
Australian
252 George St
02 9240 3010

Est is everything you'd expect from a restaurant that received three prestigious chefs hats from *The Sydney Morning Herald Good Food Guide*. This is a very glamorous dining experience. You could start with a lobster soup with snow peas, black fungi, lemongrass and kaffir lime for $33. Then follow with a pan-roasted John Dory fillet for $47, finishing off with the caramelised French toast for $22.   Wynyard, Map p.228 B2 **13**

glass brasserie
French
488 George St
02 9265 6068

You get an inkling that you're about to experience something special as you're welcomed into the striking earth-coloured dining room, even if your table isn't beside the floor to ceiling window overlooking the QVB. But, it's the food that really steals the show. Entrees start at $17.50 for half a dozen oysters, while a main of fig tart will set you back about $23.50. There's also an extensive winelist.   Town Hall, Map p.231 F3 **14**

Grand Taverna
Spanish
Cnr Liverpool and George Sts
02 9267 3608

Those in the know flock here for cheap Spanish eats over a cold brew, whether it's a local beer or a jug of sangria ($16). The tasty tapas of marinated baby octopus, barbecue and spicy prawns and garlic mushrooms is a popular choice as a shared starter, as is the $28 banquet as a main. Museum, Map p.233 F1 **15**

Hellenic Club
Greek
251-253 Elizabeth St   02 9264 5792
Escape the rush and enjoy the Hyde Park view over a lengthy lunch or relaxing dinner. You can tuck into a three-course meal here for $27.50 and entrees start at just $6. If you want good Greek super quick, line up at the bistro before settling into a game of pool with friends. Museum, Map p.234 A3 **16**

Industrie – South of France
French
107 Pitt St   02 9221 8001
With its sexy, contemporary interior of exposed brick walls, ambient lighting and industrial-inspired furnishings, Industrie is a cool spot for breakfast, lunch, dinner or just a drink. The all-day menu is available until midnight and has dishes that offer French with a pan Mediterranean flavour. The cheese board, however, is true bleu. Wynyard, Map p.234 A2 **17**

Malay Chinese Takeaway
Malaysian
64 Castlereagh St   02 9232 7838
This is some of the best Malay Chinese food in Sydney, but it's no place for an intimate dinner. Then again, at these prices, you won't really care, and it's BYO with no corkage fee. The faded paintwork becomes unimportant once your $10 laksa is served up. It's cash all the way at this family-run restaurant, with no cards of any type accepted. Martin Place, Map p.234 A2 **18**

Miltons
25 Bligh St
Mediterranean
02 9232 0007

With its long, white, leather bench seats, crisp linen tablecloths and ambient lighting, Miltons would be the ideal backdrop for a sexy music video. It's a favourite with tourists and locals, and spreads its charm over two levels. Upstairs is for private dining and pre-dinner cocktails, while downstairs is the main eating space. Here, classic meets contemporary with warm timber finishes, marble and limestone, creating an ambience to match the Mediterranean cuisine. Try starting with an antipasto plate of marinated seafood, vegetables and cured meat from $17 and don't miss out on the saffron risotto with king prawns, calamari, black mussels and clams for $30.

Martin Place, Map p.234 A1 [19]

Prime Restaurant
1 Martin Place
Steakhouse
02 9229 7777

The sandstone interior, with large leather bucket seats and crisp tablecloths sets the stage for a truly chic and unique experience. Recognised for its excellence, the steak here is served just how it should be and there's a sommelier on hand to help you match a wine to your meal. Non-carnivores can choose from the ample seafood offerings. Martin Place, Map p.231 F2 [20]

Purple Sneakers
Cnr Abercrombie and Broadway
Nightclub
02 9211 3486

Think jam-packed dance floors, sweaty bodies and a house party vibe and you"ll have an idea of what Purple Sneakers is all about. It's a cheap night out with a cover charge of just

$10. With everything from hip hop to rock, electro, indie and disco this place caters to a broad selection of Sydney's music loving crowd. Central, Map p.233 D3 **21**

The Slip Inn
Pub
111 Sussex St
02 9240 3000

Those who know will tell you The Slip Inn has a fairytale to tell. It was here during the 2000 Olympics that Aussie girl Mary Donaldson met Frederick; the Crown Prince of Denmark and her future husband. Stylish and brimming with city slick, The Slip Inn boasts bars, a lounge, club area and, if you work up an appetite, good food. Wynyard, Map p.231 E2 **22**

Tank
Nightclub
3 Bridge Lane
02 8295 9966

Tank is swimming with cool tunes and a crowd to match. The three bars, two dance floors and VIP area are a second home to keen clubbers and the international DJ's who entertain them. To keep up with the young, sophisticated crowd, you'll need to dress the part – it's funky jeans and sneakers all the way here. Circular Quay, Map p.228 B1 **23**

Tetsuya's
Japanese
529 Kent St
02 9267 2900

Tetsuya's reputation precedes itself. You often need to book months in advance to secure a place at this much talked about Franco/Japanese experience. The two elegantly plush dining rooms fittingly overlook a Japanese garden.
 Town Hall, Map p.233 E1 **24**

Going Out

Circular Quay & The Rocks

Going Out

It's all about the views, cocktails and swanky food down in these sparkling docks. Wherever you choose, it seems every table offers a glimpse of the bridge or the Opera House.

This part of town is popular with both tourists and swanky city types and bars and restaurants are priced accordingly. Antwhere with a terrace on the quay itself is likely to be packed at all times, and with such a turnover of punters, value (and service) can sometimes suffer.

But, there is a reason why people are prepared to pay a little more round here, and there are a number of spots that are well worth the extra dollars.

Venue Finder

Ocean Room	Contemporary	p.173
Bilson's Restaurant	French	p.171
Guillaume at Bennelong	French	p.172
Yoshii	Japanese	p.173
harbourkitchen&bar	Mediterranean	p.172
The Blu Horizon Bar	Bar	p.171
Bubble	Bar	p.171
ECQ	Bar	p.172
MCA Café	Cafe	p.173

Bilson's Restaurant

French
02 8214 0496

27 O'Connell St

You're allowed to have high expectations when it comes to Bilson's, which sits in the foyer of the Radisson Plaza. The restaurant's romantic surroundings make it a great choice for first dates, with its calm lighting and attentive yet unobtrusive service. The whole experience may make you feel like a million dollars, but you don't have to part with last week's wages to come here. Martin Place, Map p.228 C3 **25**

The Blu Horizon Bar

Bar
02 9250 6000

Shangri-La Hotel, 176 Cumberland St

The cocktails waiting at the top of the Shangri-La Hotel are well worth the 36-storey ride. While hotel guests make up much of the clientele, it's also a popular spot with Sydneysiders. You can order one of 300 cocktails, mixed to perfection by the world champion flair bartender and a team of mixologists. It's worth paying that bit extra for the spectacular views. Circular Quay, Map p.226 B4 **26**

Bubble Champagne Cocktail Lounge

Bar
02 9251 0311

18 Opera Quays

Sydney's first and only dedicated champagne lounge, Bubble is home to 30 of the best varieties, making it a must-visit for its sumptuous cocktails. The A-listers, suits and eastern suburb socialites flock here for its signature cocktail, Bubblicious – a mix of Plymouth gin, raspberries, lemon juice and a touch of sugar, topped with champagne. With its Circular Quay view, Bubble is a top spot for a fun night. Circular Quay, Map p.227 D2 **27**

Sydney **mini** Explorer

ECQ Bar

Bar

Quay Grand, 63 Macquarie St   02 9256 4000

It's swanky but not too pompous at the ECQ Bar. Choose from the extensive wine and cocktail list as you order from the delicious $26 tapas menu, which features chargrilled Turkish bread, guacamole, tapenade, marinated olives and all of the usual trimmings. For those who get the midnight munchies over a glass of chilled ale, you can also order the more filling wedges and sour cream. Circular Quay, Map p.227 E4 **28**

Guillaume at Bennelong

French

Opera House   02 9241 1999

Housed in the southern shell of the Sydney Opera House, the menu offers plenty of mouth-watering reasons as to why this restaurant wins so many awards. Food here is mod Oz with a classical French influence. Opt for a romantic dinner for two in the intimate booths or at a private dining table. Otherwise, gather with friends over canapes at the bar before settling into the curved bench seats. St James, Map p.227 F2 **29**

harbourkitchen&bar

Mediterranean

7 Hickson Rd   02 9256 1661

With its views over the Opera House, you'll need to book well in advance to secure a table at this delightful restaurant in the Park Hyatt hotel. Whether you choose to lunch the day away, or soak up the sunset over dinner, it's hard to imagine ever being disappointed in this restaurant, with its floor to ceiling glass windows, impeccable service and modern menu of Mediterranean-inspired flavours. Circular Quay, Map p.226 C1 **30**

MCA Café   Cafe
140 George St   02 9241 4253

This is alfresco dining at its finest. People watch, with the Opera House as a backdrop, as you dig into freshly shucked oysters and sip on well chosen wines. This is consistently popular with lunchtime crowds, so it's a good idea to prebook. If it's just a coffee you're after, try it over a dessert. Entrees at MCA Café start at $18 and mains at $25. Circular Quay, Map p.226 C3 **31**

Ocean Room   Contemporary
Overseas Passenger Terminal   02 8273 1277

Everything about this restaurant is inspired by the ocean, from the clever modern design, with a live aquarium wall, to the beautifully presented menu. Combined with the knockout harbour view, it's easy to see why the Ocean Room is so popular. Come for Japanese staples such as sushi and sashimi, with rich Mediterranean flavours - try the tuna, poached in olive oil with kaffir salad, or the $90 per head tasting menu if you really can't decide. Circular Quay, Map p.227 D2 **32**

Yoshii   Japanese
115 Harrington St   02 9247 2566

There's passion in the food at this beautifully decked out restaurant, from the lunch and dinner menus to the sushi bar. Tokyo-born chef Yoshii Ryuichi marries the traditional with the modern by serving up dishes like Japanese yam braised in rice water and bonito stock (that's dried fish flakes), served with shavings of foie gras and duck mince. The popular sushi bar menu starts at $100. Circular Quay, Map p.226 B4 **33**

Darling Harbour & Chinatown

While Darling Harbour is all fabricated glitz, neighbouring Chinatown is a little earthier and generally much cheaper.

Darling Harbour was largely derided by locals when it emerged, 10 years ago, from its redevelopment. And, while parts of it can look a little tacky, a number of good bars and restaurants have since opened up, to make this one of the city's most popular areas for wining and dining. If you chose a spot with a view of the sparkling harbour lights, you may well wonder what they got so upset about.

Over in Chinatown, things are a little scruffier, cheaper and less fabricated. The pedestrian strip of Dixon Street, which runs down to Paddy's Markets, is lined with Chinese restaurants. These all generally turn out good quality food, but as in cities across the world, the surest indication that a place is worth visiting (and a bit authentic) is the number of Chinese people eating inside.

Venue Finder

The Front	Contemporary	p.175
Zaaffran	Indian	p.177
Chinta Ria	Malaysian	p.175
Sumac	Middle Eastern	p.176
Ice Cube	Seafood	p.176
The Loft Bar	Bar	p.176
Home	NIghtclub	p.175

Chinta Ria, Temple of Love
201 Sussex St

Malaysian
02 9264 3211

It's busy at Chinta Ria. It doesn't matter what day of the week it is, you'll witness (along with the gigantic Buddha in the entrance), hoards of hungry diners looking for a decent Malaysian meal without an exorbitant price tag. Considering its prime location, with stunning views of Cockle Bay, it's a great deal. While the basic seating and chatter from nearby diners might not keep you there for hours on end, the authentic dishes will ensure you come again.   Town Hall, Map p.231 E4 **34**

The Front Restaurant and Bar
11 Hickson Rd, Walsh Bay

Contemporary
02 8298 9999

Tucked away from the hurried crowds at The Rocks nearby, The Front Restaurant and Bar at The Sebel Pier One is romantic fine dining without the pomp, with views out over Walsh Bay. For $60 you can savour perfectly seared scallops with smoked salmon and tempura avocado, slow roasted lamb shank with kumara mash followed by chocolate cherry bombe dessert. There's also an impressive selection of Australian wines.   Circular Quay and 431, Map p.226 A1 **35**

Home
Cockle Bay

Nightclub
02 9266 0600

Home is Sydney's superclub. As weekends roll around, a sea of drinkers and dancers fill the multilevel main room, but for a chilled cocktail and a break from the beats, they hit the 'padded cell', silver room. Internationally renowned DJ's fill the roster from Thursday to Saturday nights. The views from the roof terrace make for a refreshing break from the largeness downstairs. Home also stages regular gay events, including 'Queer Nation' parties. 🚇 Darling Park, Map p.231 E4 **87**

Ice Cube Seafood Grill Bar
Seafood
Imax, 31 Wheat Rd 02 8267 3666

Even at full capacity, the service at Ice Cube is as slick as the interior. Just when you think the Ice Cube experience couldn't get better – out comes the food. The taster plate starter at just $20 per head is full of fresh, perfectly pan-cooked seafood. The mains continue to please, and don't leave without a serving of tiramisu. If you love to people watch, arrive early and have a drink at the adjacent Ice Cube Bar. 🚇 Town Hall, Map p.231 E4 **37**

The Loft Bar
Bar
3 Lime St, King Street Wharf 02 9299 4770

The Loft Bar is as well dressed as its beautiful clientele. Laze back into large leather sofas with your drink in hand, surrounded by dazzling, light-filled, timber panelled walls and Sydney water views. The Loft's cocktail selections are endless and take their inspiration from flavours of the Middle East, Mediterranean, Far East and the Americas - the eastern breakfast martini is a must. 🚇 Wynyard, Map p.231 E2 **38**

Sumac
Middle Eastern
The Promenade 02 9281 2700

Tastes of the Mediterranean, Middle East and north Africa collide in a flavour explosion at Sumac. Swipe just-baked Turkish bread through mounds of plentiful dips on a mezze plate that also boasts chargrilled quail and superb vine leaves. If the bread and dips aren't enough for you, try the fried almond crumbed haloumi in quince sauce. If you're after a quiet meal, it's best to come here for lunch. Harbourside, Map p.231 D3 88

Zaaffran — Indian
345 Harbourside Shopping Ctr — 02 9211 8900

If you adore good (affordable) Indian food, look no further than Zaaffran. Set in Darling Harbour, with glorious Cockle Bay views, the restaurant is easy to reach by foot or ferry should you choose to linger over a few glasses of wine. Perfect for an intimate dinner or a bigger get together, Zaaffran is a vegetarian's paradise, with a big percentage of its menu dedicated to vegan fare. Meat lovers will rave about the free-range chicken tandoori. Harbourside, Map p.231 D3 40

Kings Cross & Woolloomooloo

Kings Cross houses brothels, strip clubs and trendy bars, all wedged between the sophistication of Potts Point and Woolloomooloo.

Kings Cross is perhaps the seediest part of Sydney. It might also be the most fun. While prostitution and drugs are highly visible, so are the police, and the ultra bohemian air has attracted many bar owners and revellers. Woolloomooloo is a little quieter, and has benefitted from the conversion of the finger wharf into a nightime hub for genteel diners and drinkers. Over in Potts Point, there are some very glam places tucked away in the leafy side streets.

Venue Finder

Aperitif	Australian	p.179
China Doll	Chinese	p.180
Hugo's Bar Pizza	Italian	p.181
Arun Thai	Thai	p.179
The Bourbon	Bar	p.179
Iguana Bar & Restaurant	Bar	p.181
Harry's Café de Wheels	Cafe	p.180
Yellow Bistro	Cafe	p.182
Club 77	Gay & Lesbian	p.180
Ladylux	Nightclub	p.181
Moulin Rouge	Nightclub	p.182
Tonic Lounge	Nightclub	p.182

Aperitif

Australian
02 9357 4729

7 Kellett St

This sleek bar and restaurant, neatly tucked away, is for those who want to combine outstanding sommelier-chosen wines with great food. You can match these to dishes such as Claire de Lune Sydney rock oysters, a substantial paella of Spanish rice with chicken and seafood or the grilled mussels, tomato, saffron and pimientos. The kitchen stays open well past midnight. Kings Cross, Map p.235 E4 **41**

Arun Thai

Thai
02 9326 9135

28 Macleay St

Loyal fans have been coming to this relaxed haven to escape the busy streets of Potts Point for two decades. Arrive early to enjoy Thai tapas and drinks at the bar area, before being seated by the attentive staff at linen-clothed tables. For those who're after a hit of true Thai spice, the pla nung manow, from the chef's signature menu selection, is a must-try. Vegetarians are well catered for too. Kings Cross, Map p.235 E4 **42**

The Bourbon

Bar
02 9358 1144

24 Darlinghurst Rd

It's all about polished pub grub and people watching at this once rundown Kings Cross favourite. Locals love the $10 lunches, which guarantee a feed of 250-gram prime rib, fries or mash, a choice of sauces and a green salad. The modern seating, in fresh hues of lime and chocolate with splashes of red, is quickly filled when $3 happy hour arrives, from Monday to Thursday between 18:00 and 21:00. Kings Cross, Map p.235 E4 **89**

China Doll
6 Cowper Wharf Rd

Chinese
02 9380 6744

There's something about this place on Sydney's historic finger wharf that makes you want to roll your lunch into dinner. The calming Iain Halliday-designed decor, the city skyline view and the well-proportioned modern Asian dishes served up by attentive staff combine to make the China Doll experience beautiful. Considering its well-to-do location, prices here don't hurt as much as you might expect.

Kings Cross and 111, Map p.235 D3 44

Club 77
77 William St

Gay & Lesbian
02 9361 4981

This small, smokey club has been on the go for over ten years now and is something of a Sydney institution. Open til late from Thursday to Sunday, it fills up quickly and gets pretty hot so don't overdo the layers. Tunes swing towards the alternative. Celebs have been known to pop in from time to time, and Lily Allen has performed here. Kings Cross, Map p.234 C4 45

Harry's Café de Wheels
Cowper Wharf Rd

Cafe
02 9357 3074

This 60-year-old icon has fed many an A-lister, tourist and local with its authentic meat pies with mash and peas, as well as hot dogs and pasties. On the walls you'll see its colourful history, full of photographs of the celebrities who've been there. Don't expect five-star cuisine from this must-visit eatery – it's plastic knives and forks all the way. Shutters stay open 24 hours. Kings Cross, Map p.235 D2 46

Hugo's Bar Pizza
Italian
33 Bayswater Rd
02 9357 4411

Rub shoulders with the hip crowd at this classy hangout and enjoy what may well be the best pizza you've ever had. Dubbed home to 'the world's best' at the 2005 New York Pizza Challenge, Hugo's is about more than just good Italian pie. Catch up with pals in the cosy sunken lounge area, complete with fireplace, or liven it up with a rhubarb and star anise cocktail at the onyx bar. Kings Cross, Map p.237 E1 **47**

Iguana Bar and Restaurant
Bar
15 Kellett St
02 9357 2609

In colourful Kings Cross, with its bright lights and ladies of the night, sits the Iguana Bar. It's the perfect spot for those looking for a filling Aussie meal, a late night snack or just a drink at the dimly lit bar. Considered a city celebrity haven since way back, you can check out the photo evidence plastered to the walls. Local fare, from kangaroo to barramundi, is on the menu. Kings Cross, Map p.235 E4 **48**

Ladylux
Nightclub
2 Roslyn St
02 9361 5000

The first thing that hits you about Ladylux is the gloriously garish mock flock wallpaper. The pink, Florence Broadhurst designed floral swirls make the place look lavish and trendy, while the dinky little alcoves are grand spots to cosy up and chat and drink. The dancefloor also sees a lot of action. Nights vary through the week, with a tendency towards funky house, and international DJs play regularly. Kings Cross, Map p.235 E4 **49**

Sydney **mini** Explorer

Moulin Rouge

Nightclub

39 Darlinghurst Rd 02 8345 1711

Everyone is happy at Moulin Rouge, a cool and homely underground nightclub in the depths of Kings Cross. As with most worthy nightspots in Sydney, you can expect to join the lengthy queue before you're granted entry. But once you're in, the sexy vibe and inviting, eclectic surrounds reminiscent of its Parisian namesake will make you forget all about the short wait. Head here for Rouge Rock-R every Friday and DJ sounds of Moulin Nights every Saturday. Kings Cross, Map p.235 E4 **50**

Tonic Lounge

Nightclub

62-64 Kellett St 02 8354 1544

This club fills a charming, two-storey terrace house with shabby chic and Victorian grandeur. But you won't be frowned on if you're not as well styled yourself. The friendly staff are fond of sharing the good times, often making their own DJ requests and dancing when the mood takes. In between dances, you can sit back with a well mixed martini in one of the velvet booths. Kings Cross, Map p.235 E4 **51**

Yellow Bistro & Food Store

Cafe

57 Macleay Street 02 9357 3400

The walls are certainly yellow here, but it's more than just the paintwork that makes this place shine. A slice of homemade pie will cost you around $13 but every last mouthful is worth it. Washed down with a perfectly brewed coffee, or a good glass of wine, it's easy to lose a couple of hours here. Vegetarians are well catered for. Kings Cross, Map p.235 E4 **52**

Going Out

Going Out

Manly

This laid back beachside suburb is a little less flash than Bondi, and offers a range of great restaurants, from Spanish, to seafood to African.

Manly is the archetypial Aussie seaside suburb, and many feel that its relaxed vibe is more 'true blue' than fashion conscious Bondi. It's main entertainment venues are spread out in a rough 'H', with the pedestrianised Corso forming the horizontal, and the two beachside strips the uprights. The East and West Esplanades either side of the Manly Wharf have venues that are instantly recognisable to Sydneysiders, most notable the Manly Wharf Hotel. Over on the North and South Steynes behind Manly Beach, the venues offer casual class, away from the typical seaside town offerings found on The Corso.

Venue Finder

Out of Africa	African	p.187
Manly Phoenix	Chinese	p.185
Will & Toby's	Italian	p.186
Manly Wharf Hotel	Mediterranean	p.189
Jellyfish	Seafood	p.185
Alhambra	Spanish	p.185
Bathers' Pavilion	Cafe	p.186

Alhambra Café and Tapas Bar

Spanish
54 West Esplanade   02 9976 2975

Pull up a pew and dine alfresco at Alhambra, as Manly's famous ferries pull up just outside. Inside, flamboyant flamenco dancers and Spanish guitarists entertain a happy crowd from Thursday to Saturday. The food, prepared using the best of Moroccan and Spanish know-how, is also worth celebrating. You can sample the Charmoula sardines for just $14. Or try the chargrilled swordfish with olive and caper salsa for $26.

Manly Ferry Wharf, Map p.242 A2 **53**

Jellyfish

Seafood
93-95 North Steyne   02 9977 4555

Manly locals love Jellyfish for its casual class. Here, eating a breakfast of smoked salmon and eggs is an experience rather than just a meal and one coffee will never be enough. Come dinner, the ocean views go perfectly with the menu of fresh seafood. The experience is made all the more enjoyable thanks to the friendly, upbeat staff who would never hurry you from your seat, despite the eager patrons looming in line.

Manly Ferry Wharf, Map p.242 C1 **54**

Manly Phoenix

Chinese
Manly Wharf, East Esplanade   02 9977 2988

The modern Chinese served here is as good as the view. The famous wharf lends itself perfectly to a relaxed meal over $24 yum cha or, for those who choose to linger longer, the $88 taster menu. The Singapore chilli snow crab is good or, if you don't mind a bit of a kick, the beef fillet cubes with wasabi sauce are excellent. Sample some of the well-chosen in-house wines and take the ferry, bus or jet cat home.

Manly Ferry Wharf, Map p.242 B2 **90**

Bathers' Pavilion
Cafe
4 The Esplanade, Balmoral Beach
02 9969 5050

Bathers' Pavilion is considered as much a city landmark as the Harbour Bridge. Once a changing shed for swimmers, it's now a welcoming haven of private dining rooms with an a la carte restaurant, bar and cafe. Of a weekend, the latter bustles with hungry brunchers who are more than willing to perch at the bar to wait for the next table. Try the eggs Benedict, which are possibly the best in Sydney. This is one restaurant you'll be back to again. North Sydney and **230**

Will & Toby's
Italian
8-13 South Steyne
02 9977 5944

There's nothing fish and chips about this seaside restaurant, with its impeccable service, tantalising menu and wines to match. Brothers Will and Toby, who opened their first bistro and bar in Darlinghurst five years ago, have excelled themselves in Manly with an open, airy venue that makes the most of the beach view. Its whitewashed walls and comfy bench seats are relaxing, so take your time as you choose from the modern menu. Whether you want the full dining experience, or just to wander off the sand for a bite to eat, the real showstoppers here are the desserts, such as the frozen pistachio nougatine with candied zest and fresh fruit.

Manly Ferry Wharf, Map p.242 C3 **57**

Manly Wharf Hotel
East Esplanade, Manly Wharf

Mediterranean
02 9977 1266

To some, the Manly Wharf Hotel is as famous as the green and yellow ferries that dock near its door. Grab one of the large timber outdoor tables and place your order for a pizza, $15, or stick with the sea theme and choose the tender salt and pepper squid, $14, or fish and chips, $19. Kids are also well catered for, with a special 'little ones' menu with goodies such as mini cheese and tomato pizza. Manly Ferry Wharf, Map p.242 A2 58

Out of Africa
43-45 East Esplanade

African
02 9977 0055

The north African cuisine here is excellent, served as you sit on brightly coloured cushions in the seaside suburb of Manly. There's an extensive menu of Moroccan favourites, including a meatball tagine that is simmered in a flavour-filled tomato sauce, with onion, garlic, spices and poached eggs. Expect to pay around $24 for an ample main. Manly Ferry Wharf, Map p.242 B3 59

Going Out — Manly

Going Out: Newtown

Newtown typifies the inner wests 'alternative' vibe and couldn't be more different from the glamourous, outdoorsy lifestyle found to the east.

This is where to come for homemade ginger beer, soy nuggets and chefs that work marvels with tofu. It's got more organic options than you can shake a lentil at, all mixed in with some rough and ready pubs and an icon of Sydney's gay scene. Such is the popularity of this former working class district, that the bars and restaurants are spilling further down King Street and Enmore Road into Erskineville and Enmore. You're as likely to see faux punks and raging queens as new age hippies and white collar yuppies in this melting pot of urban Sydney life.

Venue Finder

African Feeling	African	p.189
Kafenes	Greek	p.191
Steki Taverna	Greek	p.191
Arabella	Middle Eastern	p.189
Newton's Cucina	Mexican	p.191
Green Gourmet	Vegan	p.190
Green Palace	Vegetarian	p.190
Bank Hotel	Gay & Lesbian	p.189

African Feeling

African
501 King St
02 9516 3130

Chug back a homemade ginger beer as you settle into this small, cosy restaurant in the heart of alternative Newtown. With unfamiliar aromas wafting from the kitchen you may well forget you're in Australia. Roll your own fufu balls (mashed yams) while tapping your toes to the constant beats of the African drum. Dishes here cover traditional and modern African, with recipes from around the continent. Bring friends along to feast on the $30 banquet, or make it a dinner for two over an entree of corn bread and butter for just $6.50, followed by the West African spinach stew for $13.50. Non-meat eaters can get their fill with the vegetarian jungle, a combination of three veggie dishes. St Peters, Map p.241 A4 60

Arabella

Middle Eastern
489-491 King St
02 9550 1119

Arabella lovingly brings a taste of Beirut to Sydney. Decked out in chic, modern style, but with a traditional cushion room, the restaurant comes alive to the beat of belly dancers on Friday and Saturday nights. While the chef will suggest you feast on a mixed grill with sides of hummus, tabbouleh and fresh Lebanese bread, the lamb shawarma is just as good. Banquets here start at $35 per person. St Peters, Map p.241 A4 60

Bank Hotel

Gay & Lesbian
324 King St
02 9557 1692

This bar cum club cum restaurant has had a multi-million dollar refurbishment. The Thai restaurant is popular and serves great food while the multi-level beer garden is great for a few drinks. The cocktails are heavenly and should get you in the mood to shake a few moves in The Velvet Room upstairs. Open Sunday to Tuesday from 10:00-00:00, Wednesday and Thursday from 10:00 till 02:00 and from 10:00 to 04:00 on Fridays and Saturdays. Newtown, Map p.241 A3

Green Gourmet

Vegan

115-117 King St 02 9519 5330

Don't expect to find meat of any kind at this vegan Asian eatery. The family-run restaurant takes pride in 'nourishing the body and mind' with freshly prepared vegan food at reasonable prices. If it's all a bit new to you, you could start with the steamed barbecue 'not pork' bun, $2.80, before moving on to the soft tofu and soy nugget, presented in a clay pot and dressed with fresh mushrooms and soy sauce for $12.80. Gluten intolerants flock here for the $5.20 desert menu such as the yummy green tea moon cake.

Macdonaldtown, Map p.241 B1

Green Palace

Vegetarian

182 King St 02 9550 5234

With its generous portions, you'll be hard pushed not to leave food on your plate at Green Palace. Thai chef Kijja Silanuluck ensures a continuous flow of loyal customers with his crispy faux duck salad and enticing curries, washed down with Thai iced tea. Cuisine here is cooked with care and served by friendly staff. You can't help but leaving Green Palace feeling more centred and zen, and very full. Macdonaldtown, Map p.241 B2

Kafenes
Greek

149 Enmore Rd
02 9557 7580

Traditional to the core, this busy restaurant serves up all the favourites like moussaka, souvlaki and loukanika complemented by authentic Greek salads. A short stroll from the popular Enmore Theatre, if you don't have time to compete with the crowds, be sure to plan your visit for when there aren't any shows on. But even at peak periods, the service is fast and friendly. Newtown, Map p.241 off A3 **65**

Newton's Cucina
Mexican

403 King St
02 9519 8211

While Newton's may not sound like its roots began anywhere close to Mexico, don't let the name fool you. From the fajitas to the nachos, the food here is as authentic as you'll get in Sydney, a city where good Mexican restaurants are hard to find. Servings are generous enough to share, with mains hovering around $29. And although the dishes may be Mexican, you won't find sombrero-clad walls. Newtown, Map p.241 A3 **66**

Steki Taverna
Greek

2 O'Connell St
02 9516 2191

It's loud and fabulously festive inside Steki Taverna, with its live entertainment and excitable customers. You won't leave hungry whether you opt for the seafood platter, or the tender, slow-cooked lamb. If, after a dance on the nearby stage, you've worked up a second hunger, you can opt for the traditional bougatsa (a filo wrapped semolina custard with icing sugar and cinnamon). Newtown, Map p.241 B1 **67**

Sydney **mini** Explorer

Going Out

North Sydney

North Sydney is a business enclave that can be very quiet after office hours. But, it's also home to successful young families and considered a little 'old money'. As a result, there are some quite sophisticated spots hidden away.

North Sydney is often overlooked by visitors, the sparkiling harbour seeming too much of an obstacle. But it's worth a look, and has a distinctly different feel to the rest of the city. To the south and east of North Sydney station lay Milsons Point and Kirribilli. The latter houses the Prime Minister's official residence and has a cute, village feel. The Kirribilli pub, which can be seen from the eastern exit of Milsons Point Station is a pleasant drinking den with a well stocked bottle shop next door. Up in North Sydney proper many places close in the evenings, once the office crowd has gone home. But, there are a few gems that stay open to serve the locals with an international array of foods.

Venue Finder

Haroo	Korean	p.193
Garfish	Seafood	p.193
Nu's	Thai	p.193
The Firehouse	Bar	p.193

The Firehouse
Bar
86 Walker St
02 8904 9696

While North Sydney can seem like a ghost town at night, the full rooms of The Firehouse suggest they've all come here to enjoy dinner or the $14 cocktails. You can sit in the garden, or balcony, or head down to the cocktail lounge, with its comfortable sofas and leather stools. North Sydney, Map p.240 A1 **91**

Garfish
Seafood
2/21 Broughton St
02 9922 4322

From the snapper pie to the spanner crab with basil gnocchi, you're guaranteed freshness without fuss at Garfish. Specialising in lesser-known fish has ensured a roaring and returning trade. It's rare to find an empty seat, either inside or outside and breakfast is also very popular. Milsons Point, Map p.240 B3 **69**

Haroo
Korean
155 Miller St
02 9922 1993

Korean at heart with a hint of Japanese, Haroo is small in size, but big on taste. A good spot for lunch or an intimate dinner. Most tables have traditional barbecues, and the extensive menu has some of the best tempura in town. North Sydney, Map p.240 A1 **70**

Nu's
Thai
178 Blues Point Rd
02 9954 1780

The $9 Thai tapas is a great way to start your culinary excursion here, as you ponder a menu that features dishes of deep fried snapper, chargrilled scallops and wok-fried pork hock. The service here is fast and friendly. North Sydney, Map p.240 off A2 **71**

Sydney mini Explorer

Surry Hills & Darlinghurst

Darlinghurst is Sydney's capital of camp, while Surry Hills is developing as the city's new foodie fantasy.

The Darlinghurst action tends to centre on Oxford street, with gay and straight venues side by side. A number of cooler, less in-your-face venues can be found off this main drag, in the direction of Kings Cross, along long side streets like Liverpool and Victoria. For the main restaurant action, head to Crown Street in Surry Hills. This area has developed from a somewhat dreary inner city suburb to become Sydney's new dining hotspot.

Venue Finder

Billy Kwong	Chinese	p.195
Kirketon	Contemporary	p.197
Oh! Calcutta!	Indian	p.198
Café Mint	Middle Eastern	p.195
Casapueblo	South American	p.196
Govinda's	Vegetarian	p.197
The Victoria Room	Bar	p.199
Bills	Cafe	p.195
The Columbian Hotel	Gay & Lesbian	p.196
Slide	Gay & Lesbian	p.198
Ruby Rabbit	Nightclub	p.198
The Clock Hotel	Pub	p.196
Green Park Hotel	Pub	p.197

Bills

Cafe
433 Liverpool St 02 9360 9631

Mention this iconic cafe to any knowing Sydneysider, and the word you're most likely to hear is 'breakfast'. Whether it's to catch-up with friends or to have a business meeting, Bills is a regular hangout. The perfect scrambled eggs ($11.80) and sweet corn fritter with roast tomato, spinach and bacon ($16.80), will take you through to dinnertime. With two other Bills outlets in Surry Hills and Woollahra, its never been easier to get in on the action. Kings Cross, Map p.237 E1 **72**

Billy Kwong

Chinese
355 Crown St 02 9332 3300

If you're not too concerned about a lack of elbowroom or perching on stools, it's worth the wait to score a table at this tiny eatery. Owner, chef and media personality Kylie Kwong has successfully married organic and biodynamic Chinese cuisine with Sydney swank. Over a glass of BYO wine, order the banquet to really get a taste for what the fuss is all about.
 Central, Map p.236 B3 **73**

Café Mint

Middle Eastern
579 Crown St 02 9319 0848

It really doesn't matter about the lack of space at Café Mint – it's the menu that grabs your attention. Settle in with a glass of BYO on the bench seating, before perusing a menu that boasts an eclectic mix of Middle Eastern fare. Start with the mezze plate of gourmet dips, followed by one of the delicious mains. Café Mint opens early, with those in the know clambering to get a taste of the breakfast couscous, for $10.90. Central and 395, Map p.236 off B4 **74**

Casapueblo
South American
474 Cleveland St 02 9319 6377

This busy restaurant is a slice of South America in Sydney. Start with the tapas, which can include anything from potatoes with peanuts, cheese and chilli to crumbed mussels stuffed with spice. Move on to a beef, chicken and corn casserole. The chaja, a traditional meringue and cream dessert, is worth leaving room for. Central and 395, Map p.236 off B4 **75**

The Clock Hotel
Pub
470 Crown St 02 9331 5333

The Clock Hotel is always abuzz with a loyal crowd who come to mingle over drinks or for a quality meal. The food ranges from good pub grub to more sophisticated, Mediterranean-style tapas. This multi-level boozer features the relaxing Street Bar, the cool Pool Bar, and the Balcony Bar where you can sip on cocktails and be a tad more bling. There are 18 wines available by the glass here, while beer lovers can choose from bottled and premium beers on tap. Central, Map p.236 B4 **76**

The Columbian Hotel
Gay & Lesbian
117-123 Oxford St 02 9360 2151

Primarily a bar for gay men, the Columbian also attracts a significant lesbian crowd. The large windows on the ground floor are grand for gawping out and watching the world go by, or looking in and watching the lively crowd. The

bar upstairs is a little more sedate, with cosy loungers and alcoves. This is a well-liked, fairly unpretentious spot.
Museum, Map p.236 B2

Govinda's Restaurant and Cinema — Vegetarian
112 Darlinghurst Rd — 02 9380 5162

You're guaranteed to be well fed and well entertained at Govinda's, where the crowds flock to feast on plentiful vegetarian food before catching a movie in the boutique cinema. For just $16.90, you can sample the Indian menu, which always features favourites such as dal soup, vegetable curry and cauliflower pakoras. For just an extra $7.90 you'll be ushered upstairs, where you can lounge on upholstered cushions on the floor. Kings Cross, Map p.237 D1

Green Park Hotel — Pub
360 Victoria St — 02 9380 5311

This corner pub is a no-nonsense boozer with a blue-tiled, dark timbered interior and an energetic feel. It's mix of local characters, trendy eastern suburbanites and gay boys and girls. Settle in with pals and shoot some pool or enjoy a drink in the beer garden. It's open until 02:00, Monday to Saturday. Sunday afternoons here are a big tradition among the city's gay community. Kings Cross, Map p.237 D2

Kirketon Dining Room & Bar — Contemporary
207 Darlinghurst Rd — 02 9557 0770

Kirketon Dining Room and Bar is a breath of fresh air on the contemporary dining scene. Chef Jocelyn Rivière turns out

Going Out

Surry Hills & Darlinghurst

delights like beetroot and horseradish cured salmon for entree and pan-roasted ocean trout with fennel puree, broad beans, green olives and oven-dried tomatoes for main. Mains start at $28. A must-visit. Kings Cross, Map p.237 D1 80

Oh! Calcutta! — Indian
251 Victoria St — 02 9360 3650

Loyal diners have been returning to Oh! Calcutta! for almost 20 years. The saag paneer is like you've never tasted and the duck curry will melt in your mouth. First timers should try the taster menu for $47.90 per person, or the seafood option for $55 per person. Fully licensed with an ample list of local and imported beverages, you can also BYO. Kings Cross, Map p.237 D2 81

Ruby Rabbit — Nightclub
231 Oxford St — 02 9326 0044

Three storeys of sophisticated nightclub action await at Ruby Rabbit, where the cool crowd don't necessarily know it and the thirty-somethings love to show off their new moves. The Florence Broadhurst-covered walls may be narrow, but there's still plenty of room to strut your stuff and to elbow your way to the slender bar for a drink of local and imported beers, cocktails and wine. Museum, Map p.236 C3 82

Slide — Gay & Lesbian
41 Oxford St — 02 8915 1899

One of the newer additions to Sydney's strip of gay bars and clubs is Slide, housed in the Art Deco surroundings of what used to be a bank. Today it's a sophisticated Art Deco style

Ruby Rabbit

bar, club and restaurant. The young, trendy, mixed crowd make full use of the bar's split level surroundings and small, though often packed, dance floor stage. It's open until 03:00 Wednesday to Friday, and closes at 04:00 on weekends. Cover charges vary. Museum, Map p.236 B1 83

The Victoria Room
Bar
231 Victoria St www.thevictoriaroom.com

Elegantly dressed with antique leather-buttoned couches, velvet booths and splashes of brocade, you'll find dishes such as spicy Moroccan meatballs for $14 and veal melinasi for $19. This place is also known for its high tea, where Sunday brunchers come to catch up over champers and finger-sized sandwiches. The supper room is open until 01:30 for late-night dining – perfect after the theatre or movies. Kings Cross, Map p.237 D1 84

Entertainment

Sydney has more to offer than booze and food. It's a city that loves showing off, and this is reflected in the choice of shows, comedy and music available.

Cabaret & Strip Shows

It's easy to find a touch of Parisian nightlife in Sydney, with quality cabaret shows staged on sea and land. Sydney Showboats (32 The Promenade, King Street Wharf, 02 8296 7200 www.sydneyshowboats. com.au) is popular for its extravagant performances, with many of its stars having danced their way straight from the Moulin Rouge. Meanwhile, showy suburbs such as Newtown offer their very own version (think Priscilla, Queen of the Desert) in corner pubs and restaurants. The Imperial in Erskineville (34 Erskineville Rd, 02 9519 9899) was the inspiration for Priscilla, and continues to show drag acts. In Kings Cross there's a slew of adult clubs that line the famous strip (www.kingscrossonline.com.au). These range from the saucy to the seedy and many are brothels, so may not be the best spot for a giggling mixed group on a night out.

Casinos

From the grand Star City to pubs and RSL (Returned Services League) clubs lined with poker machines (pokies), it's easy and legal to place a bet in Sydney once over 18 years of age. While 2.1% of the Australian adult population has a gambling addiction, the rest spend an average of $1,000 each year trying to become instant millionaires. The largest and most popular is Star City Casino (www.starcity.com.au / 02 9777 9000) in Darling Harbour, where you can eat, sleep, drink, party and, of course, lay your wager. It's open 24 hours, so you can flutter on until dawn. While legal gambling is confined to casinos and pubs, the wartime game of two-up brings gambling to the street every ANZAC Day on April 25. It's hard not to get into the two-up spirit either, as the beer flows from early afternoon until the wee hours.

Cinemas

During the summer, outdoor cinemas are really popular. The Moonlight Cinema (www.moonlight.com.au) at Centennial Park screens classics like *Breakfast at Tiffany's* as well as new blockbusters. For a movie with a view, the open-air cinema at Mrs Macquaries Chair (www.stgeorgeopenair.com.au) at the Royal Botanic Gardens overlooks Sydney Harbour. Cinema times are listed in all the major daily newspapers and all films are rated. Dendy (www.dendy.com.au) has a few art house cinemas dotted about town, and the 17 screen Greater Union in the CBD (505-525 George St / 02 9273 7431 / www.greaterunion.com.au) will see to all your hollywood needs. See also Govinda's, on p.197.

Comedy

Aussies tend to reckon they're a witty bunch, and a number of clubs and pubs host comedy nights in Sydney. In Glebe, The Harold Park (02 9660 3688 115 Wigram Rd) is always a laugh, as is Mic in Hand (www.micinhand.com), which has developed a bit of an underground following. Held in the A Friend in Hand pub (www.friendinhand.com.au / 58 Cowper St, Glebe) this is a place where anyone can get up on stage.

Otherwise, the Fringe Bar (02 9360 5443 / www.thefringe.com.au) at 106 Oxford Street on a Monday night is hilarious, and they serve great food too. The Australian Youth Hotel (02 9692 0414 / 63 Bay Street, Glebe / www.australianyouthhotel.com.au) runs a weekly comedy night, which is always very Australian, and the perfect place to sit back and enjoy a few beers. The cream of Sydney's comedy crop though is the Laugh Garage (www.thelaughgarage.com) in Parramatta.

The Big Laugh Comedy Festival (www.biglaughriverside.com.au) runs from March 22 to April 1, overlapping with CRACKER (www.crackercomedy.com.au).

Concerts

Most major events are held at The Sydney Entertainment Centre (SEC - see table). To keep an eye on upcoming concerts, good websites include www.sonybmg.com.au, www.inthemix.com.au, www.moshtix.com.au and www.

Concerts

Art Gallery of NSW	9225 1744	www.artafterhours.com.au
Metro Theatre	9550 3666	www.metrotheatre.com.au
SEC	9320 4200	www.sydentcent.com.au
The Basement	9251 2797	www.thebasement.com.au
The Enmore Theatre	9550 3666	www.enmoretheatre.com.au
Sydney Opera House	9250 7111	www.sydneyoperahouse.com

sydneyolympicpark.com.au. The best place to see Australian bands is at grungy festivals like The Big Day Out (www.bigdayout.com), Homebake (www.homebake.com.au), Field Day (www.fuzzy.com.au) or Good Vibrations (www.goodvibrationsfestival.com.au).

Candy's Apartment (www.candys.com.au / 22 Bayswater Road / 02 9380 5600) in Kings Cross is always good for up-and-coming bands and well established local favourites. And, of course, for classical music and opera, The Opera House always has a good line up.

Theatre

From the grand Sydney Theatre Company to the Belvoir Street Theatre, there's plenty of stage action in Sydney. The city caters to all tastes – from small productions to million-dollar shows with A-list stars. Expect to pay anywhere from $15 to $80 for tickets, depending on the scale of the production. Theatre schools often put on end of term shows, at stages such as The Pilgrim, which is home to the Sydney Art Theatre. For general deals on tickets, try www.ticketmaster.com.au (no call centre) or www.showbiz.com.au (1300 658 009).

Theatre

Belvoir Street Theatre	02 9698 3344	www.belvoir.com.au
Domain Theatre	02 9225 1700	www.artgallery.nsw.gov.au
Sydney Art Theatre	02 9261 8981	www.sat.org.au
Sydney Theatre Co.	02 9250 1777	www.sydneytheatre.com.au
Theatre Royal	02 9224 8333	www.mlccentre.com.au

Profile

206 Culture
210 History
218 Sydney Today

Profile

Profile: Culture

Sydney is a young, vibrant city that throws together innumerable groups and cultures. From corporate climbers to degenerate boozers, sports nuts, surfers and artists; the whole world is here.

Sydney's culture has been formed by waves of immigration. As new citizens have arrived from southern Europe, the Middle East and Asia, the cultural links to the first immigrants - the British - have dissipated. The original colonists wanted to prove they were worthy of the mother country, but with federation came a budding sense of nationhood.

After the second world war, levels of immigration and feelings of independence increased dramatically. Most of the new arrivals first landed and settled in Sydney, and the city's culture was forever altered with large groups of Greeks, Lebanese, Maltese and Italians. A large Jewish community grew up around the Great Synagogue. The late 20th century saw increasing immigration from Asia. Each of these has left a mark on the city, from the Italian speaking shops of Leichhardt, to central Sydney's Chinatown.

So, Sydney's cultural essence, more so than the rest of Australia, is a multicultural mash up, with perhaps only a love of sport and the outdoors as an identifiable constant.

The original inhabitants of Australia, the Aborigines, have their own culture, which developed over tens of thousands of years. They refer to the creation of the world as 'Dreamtime'

The Art Gallery of New South Wales

ART GALLERY OF NEW SOUTH WALES

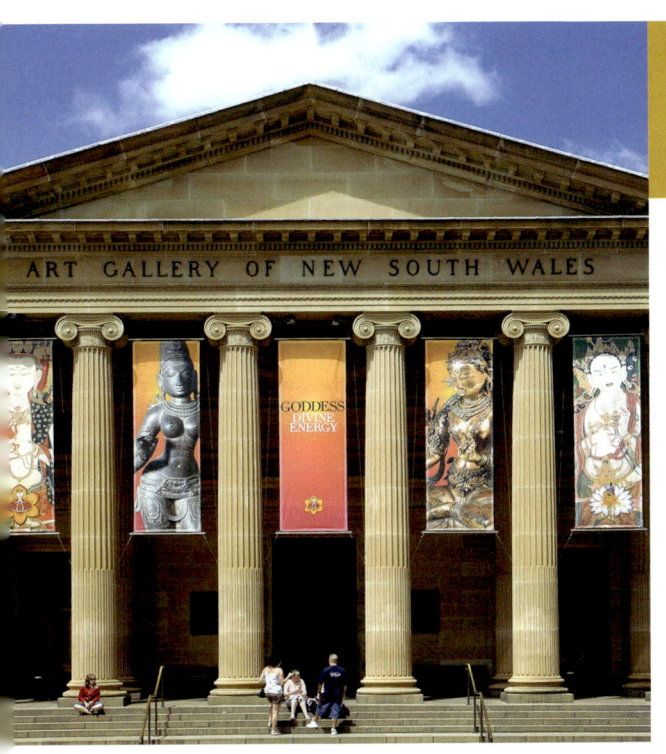

Profile

Culture

Sydney **mini** Explorer

207

(when their ancestors rose from the land to become one with nature). Aboriginal people place a profound importance on reliving and recording Dreamtime and ancestral events through traditional song, dance and rituals.

Language

The official language of Sydney is English, but on the streets you may hear anything from Afrikaans to Zulu. Visit Chinatown or even Eastwood and you could easily believe you're in downtown Hong Kong. The most common language spoken at home, other than English, is Arabic, followed by Cantonese, Greek and then Italian. Over one million people in Sydney speak languages other than English at home. There are more than 200 indigenous Australian languages but only 20 of these are actually thriving. The fast erradication of these native languages is mainly due to the fact that only 10% of the next generation are being taught them.

Strine

A true Aussie does not say 'Australian'. A true Aussie says 'Strine'. Australians also have a remarkably infectious habit of lifting the end of their sentences, as if they were asking a question. And then there's the determination to shorten names. For example, relative is shortened to 'rello', musician to 'muso', afternoon to 'arvo' and so on. The Australian approach to speech is colourful and Sydneysiders love to adapt the spoken word. Australian colloquialisms often raise vivid images, for example: 'flat out like a lizard drinking' (working very hard on a task) or 'standing like a bandicoot on a burnt ridge' (feeling lonely and vulnerable). You may feel like a bit of a 'galah' trying to figure it all out at first, but you'll soon catch on.

Food & Drink

Over the last 20 years, Aussie cuisine has developed from meat pies and lager to 'Mod Oz' and fine wine. Mod Oz is a fusion of the European and Asian influences found in the country, mixed with fresh local produce like seafood, lamb and abundant fruit and veg. But, various 'villages' within Sydney allow you to try the original elements untempered. Chinatown offers Chinese, Vietnamese, Thai, Korean and Japanese food. Ashfield is known as Little Shanghai and you can find excellent Chinese and Indian food here. Little Italy in Haberfield serves wonderful Italian food. For Lebanese dishes, visit Punchbowl, Bankstown and Lakemba. Nearby Auburn is home to many Turkish specialities. Spectacular local seafood, including fish and chips, sushi, chilli crab and freshly shucked oysters can be found at the Sydney Fish Market in Pyrmont.

Religion

Freedom of worship has been practised in Sydney since the mid 1800s. Some 30% of Sydney's population are Catholic, 20.2% are Anglican and 11.9% have no religion. The rest follow a number of spiritual paths, from Buddhism to Islam, Baptist, Sikhism and various others. As befitting the city's Christian background, the Christian calendar is followed with major celebrations at Christmas and Easter.

History

Sydney's history begins some 60,000 years before Europeans turned up.

The first Aboriginal explorers are thought to have arrived in New South Wales anywhere between 30,000 and 60,000 years ago. They were hunter-gatherers who managed the land in semi-permanent settlements and lived in separate groups with distinct languages and traditions. These groups then mingled for trade, initiations, marriages and political alliances.

The traditional owners of the Sydney City region are the Cadigal band. When asked where they came from by the British, the local Aboriginal people answered 'Eora' which means 'here' or 'from this place'. The British used the term to describe the coastal Aboriginal people found around Sydney. Central Sydney is often referred to as 'Eora Country'. Many of Sydney's main thoroughfares, such as George Street and Oxford Street, follow ancient Aboriginal tracks.

European Arrival

In 1770 Captain James Cook charted the east coast of Australia, landing at Botany Bay on April 28. He formally took possession of the eastern part of Australia in August, naming the region New South Wales. Within 20 years, the lives of the local Aboriginal people had been torn apart by disease, dispossession and social upheaval. Today, many Aboriginal people refer to the arrival of the Europeans as 'the invasion'.

On January 26 1788, the 11 ships of the First Fleet dropped anchor in Sydney Cove, marking the beginning of the

Profile

History

Sydney **mini** Explorer

settlement of Sydney. Under the command of Captain Arthur Phillip, the marines on board (along with 850 convicts) were tasked with building a prison settlement.

The local stream was soon permanently fouled. This forced the local people further out for clean drinking water. Then came the 1789 smallpox epidemic, which killed almost half of the Aboriginal community of Sydney. There were reports of bodies left floating in the harbour. By 1791 there were said to be just three Cadigal people left in the area.

The Europeans survived the smallpox but their settlement teetered on the brink of starvation. It wasn't until the Second Fleet arrived in 1790 that the colony became self-sufficient.

The Rum Corps

After Captain Phillip returned to England, the colony was administered by the New South Wales Corps (or Rum Corps, for their use of the spirit as currency) as a personal fiefdom.

Then, in 1806, Governor Bligh arrived from England. the new chief forbade the barter of spirits for food or wages and conducted a feud with the corps and John Macarthur. Bligh arrested Macarthur, who promptly persuaded the corps to mutiny. On Anniversary Day in 1808, the (well lubricated) corps marched down Bridge Street to arrest Bligh. Macarthur perched on a gun carriage and the band belted out a stirring tempo. Sydney residents, always keen on a spectacle, cheered on the mutineers. Bonfires burned effigies of Bligh and the governor was arrested. The commanding officer of the mutiny took the title of lieutenant-governor, Macarthur called himself secretary to the colony and they claimed land and convict labour for themselves and their cronies. Bligh was recalled by London and Lachlan Macquarie was dispatched with a regiment to restore order.

Macquarie, governor from 1810 to 1821, turned a rough and tumble convict station into a city with civic pride. By the time he left, Sydney had an organised police system, decent roads, a bank and a real currency. A tall Scot with a proud military background, Macquarie believed in the reformation as well as the punishment of convicts. He appointed several educated convicts to office, which scandalised the elite of the colony, especially the fiery John Macarthur. They complained bitterly to London, where authorities were concerned by the rising costs of the governor's public works.

When London sent a nitpicking official to conduct an enquiry, Macquarie saw the writing on the wall and resigned. But he won't be forgotten easily; there are more than 50 roads, streets and lanes that carry his name.

It was thanks to Macquarie's encouragement of exploration that in 1813 the Blue Mountains were conquered, opening up the interior of New South Wales. The British government granted free land, free convict labour and offered a huge market for any produce. As the colony established itself, Macquarie's civic pride prompted an ambitious programme of public works. Some of the finest buildings of the early convict period were built on his watch.

In 1842, the City of Sydney was established and representative government followed in Australia a year later.

By the mid 19th century mineral discoveries, and gold in particular, had shifted the emphasis from pastoral to mining, manufacturing and larger scale agriculture. Sydney was flooded by gold seekers and building activity boomed. In the last half of the century, Sydney exploded from 60,000 to a population of around half a million. By the end of the century, it was one of the largest cities in the western world.

Federation & Beyond

On January 1, 1901, federation was achieved and New South Wales became a state of Australia. In Sydney, slums were cleared and the city was smartened up. At this point, Aborigines were believed to be dying out and they were not included in the census of 1901 (although cattle were).

As a member of the British Empire, Australia sent 330,000 soldiers (including 300 - 500 Aborigines) to Europe during the first world war. More than 58,000 of them were killed. On April 25, 1915, the ANZACs (Australian and New Zealand Army Corps) landed on the Gallipoli Peninsula in Turkey. During the subsequent eight-month campaign, 27,000 Australian soldiers were killed or wounded. The Gallipoli legend plays a key role in the Australian psyche. This is partly to do with the bravery shown in the face of overwhelming odds, but Gallipoli also marks the start of Australia's psychological independence from Britain.

The second world war saw Australia, as a member of the British Empire and Commonwealth, at war again. This time, troops were sent to Europe, the Middle East, North Africa and the Pacific. On May 31, 1942, three Japanese midget submarines entered Sydney Harbour. A torpedo destroyed a Royal Australian Navy depot ship, killing 21 people. When America entered the war, it made Australia the Allied base in the Pacific. This was the beginning of Australia's shift in reliance on Britain to the US.

The period from the late 40s to the early 70s was an era of dramatic growth, which saw Australia's relationship with the US develop, strengthened by its involvement in the Vietnam war. By 1972 though, when Australia withdrew, economic hardships were taking their toll and the Governor-General's dismissal of the Labor government of Gough Whitlam caused the most serious constitutional crisis in Australia's history. But, the years that followed saw steady, renewed growth as John Howard's economically liberal, socially conservative government took the country into the new century.

But, it wasn't until the NSW Land Rights Act 1983 that the dispossession of indigenous Sydneysiders was finally acknowledged. The Aboriginal and Torres Strait Islander Commission (ATSIC), which acted for indigenous people on a national level, has recently been abolished.

The Stolen Generation

Until the 1960s, Aborigines fell under the control of the NSW Aborigines Welfare Board. It followed a brutally misguided policy of separating Aboriginal children from their parents in an attempt at integration. These children are known as the 'Stolen Generation'. There are between 15,000 and 20,000 of them in New South Wales.

Sydney Timeline

28,000BC to 58,000BC Aboriginal settlement
1770 Captain Cook arrives in Botany Bay
1788 European settlement begins with arrival of the First Fleet
1802 Pemulwuy, the Aboriginal resistance leader, is shot
1808 Rum Rebellion
1809 Governor Lachlan Macquarie arrives in Sydney
1813 Crossing of the Blue Mountains
1838 Myall Creek massacre – 28 Aboriginies shot by white men in northern NSW
1843 First elections
1848 Convict transportation to NSW ceased
1851 Gold rush
1893 Adult male suffrage (with restrictions for indigenous men)
1901 Federation
1902 Adult female suffrage (with restrictions for indigenous women)
1915 ANZAC lands at Gallipoli
1932 Sydney Harbour Bridge opened
1938 First 'Day of Mourning' held by Aboriginal protestors
1942 Singapore falls and 15,000 Australian troops taken prisoner. Darwin bombed and Japanese midget submarines enter Sydney Harbour

Profile

History

- **1962** Aborigines given the right to vote in Commonwealth elections
- **1965** 'Freedom Rides'. Students travel through NSW to draw attention to segregation of Aboriginal Australians
- **1967** Referendum returns overwhelming vote in favour of recognising Aborigines as Australian citizens
- **1971** Census includes Aborigines for the first time; Aboriginal flag flown for the first time
- **1972** Aboriginal 'Tent Embassy' erected outside Parliament House in Canberra
- **1973** The Sydney Opera House opens
- **1984** Advance Australia Fair becomes the national anthem and green and gold Australia's national colours. Homosexuality decriminalised
- **1987** Royal commission held into Aboriginal deaths in custody
- **1991** Council for Aboriginal Reconciliation established by an act of parliament with bipartisan support
- **1992** Sydney Harbour Tunnel opened
- **1997** Report into Stolen Generation tabled in federal parliament
- **2000** Olympic Games held in Sydney
- **2002** Bali bombing kills 88 Australians
- **2003** Iraq invasion. Australia part of 'coalition of the willing'
- **2005** Cronulla riots, between white and Muslim youths

Profile

Sydney Today

Beautiful, bustling and bursting with life, Sydney today is a city that locals feel proud of and that visitors will adore. Once here, it's easy to see why it's one of the world's great cities.

In population terms, Sydney is relatively small for a world-class city, but it's growing fast. It stretches nearly 100km from top to bottom and 55km across, making it twice the size of New York. The city is divided into four sections – geographically by north and south, socially by east and west, a relic from the settlement era. The wealthy officers generally lived in the east, while the labourers were stationed out west. Today the well-heeled still cluster among the mansions in the hilly east, while the west and southwest remain the stomping ground of the Aussie 'battlers'. The old-money north, despite its humdrum image, has some of the best beaches and protected national parks.

Multicultural Sydney

Sydney is the most multicultural city in Asia Pacific. More than 30% of residents were born overseas and that diversity helps give the city its vibrancy. But, it has also brought problems. Riots have brought international attention to the problems of Aborigines, and also highlighted the racial tensions common to other western cities since 9/11. On December 11, 2005, a riot broke out when some 5,000 people gathered to 'reclaim

Profile

the beach' from groups of Lebanese Muslim youths. Sydney's image as a tolerant, multicultural example to the world took a severe beating. However, Sydney remains an upbeat and positive city and visitors from all parts of the world will be made to feel equally welcome.

Sydney Developments

Sydney's population is predicted to grow from the current 4.2 million to 5.3 million by 2031. The government's vision for Sydney in 2031 has Sydney City and North Sydney as the heart of 'global Sydney', while the river cities of Parramatta, Liverpool and Penrith will provide more work, cultural and lifestyle opportunities. A showcase project for 'global Sydney' is the $4 billion renewal of a 22 hectare port precinct on the western edge of the CBD. Effectively, the project amounts to the regeneration of east Darling Harbour into an upmarket business and residential area. The development is expected to generate $4 billion in new investment in the state and some 30,000 jobs during the construction period of 10 years. The area will house commercial headquarters for 16,000 workers, an 11 hectare headland park and a 1.4km foreshore walk from Woolloomooloo round to the Anzac Bridge. The park is part of a continuing programme to keep the headlands free from development. The revamped area has been named Barangaroo, after the feisty wife of Bennelong, one of the First Fleet's Aboriginal contacts. Part of Hickson Road will be renamed The Hungry Mile. The name is a memorial to the desperate men that haunted the waterfront, looking for work during the Depression.

An aerial view of the harbour

Profile

Sydney Today

Maps

- **224** Sydney Overview
- **226** The Rocks
- **227** Circular Quay
- **228** CBD
- **230** Pyrmont
- **231** Darling Harbour
- **232** Glebe
- **233** Haymarket
- **234** The Domain
- **235** Kings Cross
- **236** Surry Hills
- **237** Darlinghurst
- **238** Bondi
- **240** North Sydney
- **241** Newtown
- **242** Manly
- **243** Legend
- **244** Sydney Ferries

Maps

Sydney Overview

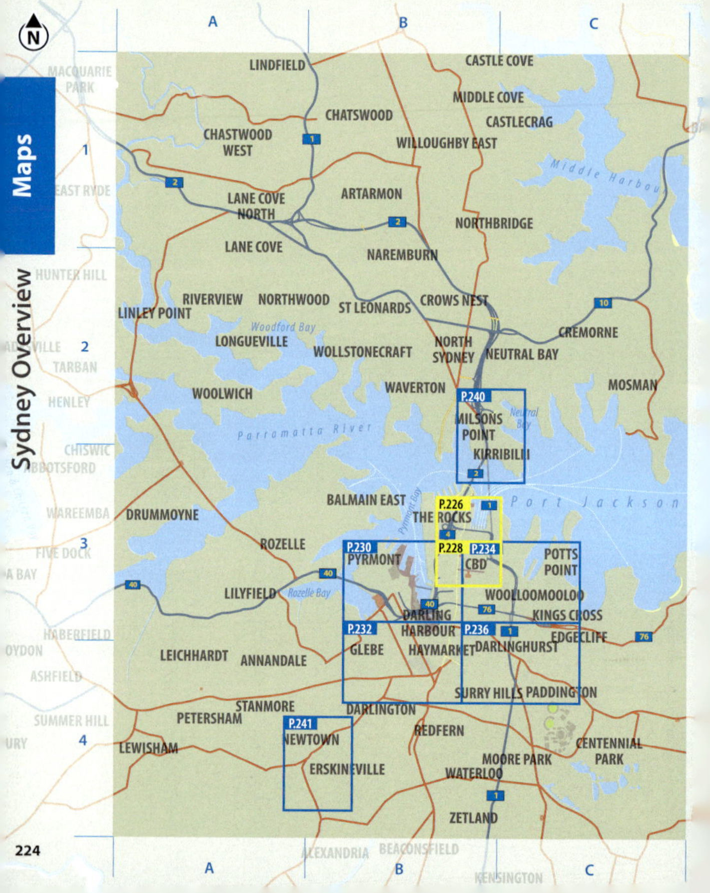

Sydney Overview

Maps

- CASTLECRAG
- BALGOWLAH
- CLONTARF
- BALGOWLAH HEIGHTS
- MANLY — P.242
- Middle Harbour
- North Harbour
- Balmoral Beach
- Tasman Sea
- CREMORNE
- NEUTRAL BAY
- MOSMAN
- Neutral Bay
- KIRRIBILLI
- FORT DENISON
- Port Jackson
- WATSONS BAY
- VAUCLUSE
- Diamond Bay
- POTTS POINT
- Rushcutters Bay
- Felix Bay
- SHARK ISLAND
- WOOLLOOMOOLOO
- KINGS CROSS
- EDGECLIFFE
- DARLINGHURST
- ROSE BAY
- DOVER HEIGHTS
- PADDINGTON
- BELLEVUE HILL
- P.238
- BONDI
- MOORE PARK
- CENTENNIAL PARK
- BONDI JUNCTION
- BONDI BEACH
- Tamarama Bay

Scale 1:10,000 — 0 – 2km

225

The Rocks

Maps

High Detail Scale — 200 m / 700 ft

Grid A

- Wharf Theatres (7, 6, 5, 4, 3) — 1
- Sydney Theatre
- Windmill St
- DAWES POINT
- Argyle Pl
- Argyle Place Park
- Observatory Park
- Sydney Observatory — 9
- National Trust Centre — 25
- The Observatory (H)

Grid B

- Hickson Rd — 35
- Pottinger St
- Lower Fort St
- Trinity Ave
- Watson Rd
- Argyle St
- Gloucester Walk
- King George V Memorial Park
- Foundation Park — 34
- Argyle Stores
- Argyle St
- Clocktower Square
- King George Rec. Centre
- Cambridge St
- Tourism House
- Gloucester St
- Susannah Place — 12
- Cumberland St
- Nurses Walk
- Globe St
- DFS Galleria
- The Terrace
- Harrington St
- Shangri-La — 26
- Canada House
- Quay West
- Four Seasons — 33

Grid C

- Bradfield Highway — 24
- Park Hyatt — 30
- Hickson Rd
- The Art Exchange
- Metcalfe Arcade
- George St
- Westpac Museum
- Old Sydney (H)
- Sydney Tourist Info
- Playfair St
- Kendall La
- Harbour Rocks (H)
- Cadmans Cottage
- Circular Quay W
- THE ROCKS
- Museum of Contemporary Art — 31
- George St
- The Russell (H) — 11
- First Fleet Park
- Cahill Expressway — 33
- Herald Square
- Alfred St
- George St
- Gold Fields House

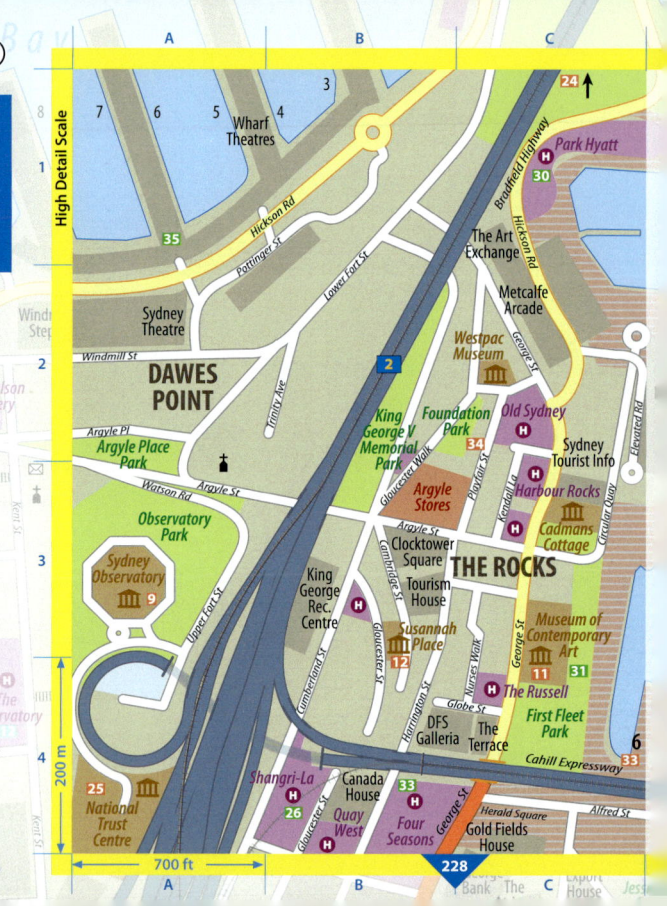

226 — 228

Circular Quay

- Dawes Point Reserve
- Campbells Cove
- Bennelong Point
- **27** Overseas Passenger Terminal **32**
- To Pyrmont Bay, Birkenhead, Parramatta, Rydalmere, Woolwich
- To Woolwich, Neutral Bay, Mosman Bay, Watsons Bay Cruises
- To Manly (p. 84)
- To Manly, Taronga Zoo, Mosman Bay, Watsons Bay
- Sydney Opera House **10 29**
- **1**
- Opera House Gate
- Government House
- Sydney Cove
- Ferry Wharves
- Circular Quay
- 5 4 3 **31** 2
- Macquarie St
- **28** Quay Grand Amatil Bldg
- Cahill Walk
- Northern Depot
- Circular Quay
- **229**
- High Detail Scale
- 200 m / 700 ft
- 227

High Detail Scale
226
231
231
A
B
C
1
2
3
4
200 m
700 ft
Cove Apts
Grosvenor Place
St George Bank
The Atrium
Export House
Sydney Harbour Marriott
Underwood House
AIG Bldg
Endeavour House
Colonial House
Lang Park
National Australia Bank House
AAP Centre
Royal Exhange Bldg
Dept of Lands
Establishment
Saville
KPMG Centre
Rydges
Corus
Australia Square Tower
Wintergarden Plaza
CGU House
Plaza Bldg
All Seasons
Grand
Radisson Plaza
Wynyard
Wynyard Park
Thakral House
Watson House
John Hunter Bldg
Rabobank House
ANZ Bank
GIO
Bank of China Bldg
Lisgar House
Bank House
CBD
Angel Place
Castlereagh Centre
Logical House
Regimental Square
Australia Chambers
Challis House
Martin Place
York Bldg
Corporation Centre
Red Cross House
Landmark Bldg
GPO
The Western Sydney
Commonwealth Bank Bldg
Cassa Comm House
Charles Plaza
NRMA House
Knight Frank
MLC Centre
Gloucester St
Harrington St
George St
Underwood St
Pitt St
Reiby Pl
Macquarie Pl
Grosvenor St
Dalley St
Bridge St
Lang St
Bridge La
Jamison St
Bent St
Bond St
Spring St
St Margaret St
O'Connell St
Hunter St
Clarence St
York La
Carrington St
Wynyard La
Erskine St
Wynyard St
Angel Pl
Hosking Pl
Castlereagh St
York St
Kent St
Martin Pl
Barrack St
King St
Western Distributor
23
13
25
National Trust
Quay West
Four
Gold Fields House
The Grace
Sydney Arcade
Westpac Place
Veritas House
Towers
Emst & You Bldg
The Chelsea
Cosco House
Sussex St

CBD

Maps

227

229

234

High Detail Scale
200 m / 700 ft

- Jessie Street Gardens
- Sydney Customs House
- Sydney Cove Bldg
- AMP Plaza
- Justice & Police Museum
- Sir Stamford at Circular Quay
- Transport House
- AMP Centre Tower
- InterContinental
- Macquarie Place Park
- Chief Sectretarys Bldg
- Museum of Sydney
- The Astor
- Education Dept Bldg
- Hudson House
- Governer Phillip Tower
- BMA House
- Governer Macquarie Tower
- Conservatorium of Music
- ABN Amro Tower
- Royal Botanic Gardens
- Norwich House
- Union Club
- The Wentworth
- Chifley Tower
- Bligh House
- Chifley Plaza
- Chifley Sq
- State Library of NSW
- Goodsell Bldg
- Colonial Centre
- Cahill Expressway
- Saving Bank Bldg
- Westpac Bldg
- Parliament House
- Martin Place
- Colonial Bldg
- BNP Paribas Centre
- Reserve Bank of Australia
- Sydney Hospital & Sydney Eye Hospital
- The Domain
- Art Gallery of NSW

Streets: Lotus St, Young St, Phillip St, Macquarie St, Bent St, Phillip La, Bligh St, Elizabeth St, Hunter St, Hospital Rd, King St, Bridge St, Tunnel

N
A
B
C
1
2
3
4
Johnstons Bay
Elizabeth Bay
Pyrmont Park
Jones Bay
Jones Bay Wharf
Darling Point
PYRMONT
Pirrama Rd
Darling Island Rd
Wharf Cr
Community Park
Pyrmont St
Refinery Dr
Mount St
Harvey St
Bowman St
John Street Square
Jones Bay Rd
Star City
Pyrmont Bay Park
Tambur St
Jones St
Cadigal Ave
John St
Harris St
Old Glebe Island Bridge
Distillery Dr
Lyric Theatre
Bank St
Anzac Bridge
4
Quarry Master Dr
Saunders St
Citywest
Union St
Miller St
TEN Studio
Western Distributor
Fish Market
Bulwara Rd
Little Mount St
Paternoster Row
Pyrmont Bridge Rd
Edward La
Harwood St
Gipps St
Bunn St
Blackwattle Bay
Blackwattle Bay Park
Bellevue Villa
Ada Pl
Experiment St
Sydney University Women's Rowing Club
Sydney Fish Market
Wattle Cr
Harris Street Motor Museum
300 m
Taylor St
Ferry Rd
Sydney Secondary College
Bridge Rd
Wentworth Park
232
1000 ft
GLEBE
Cook St
Sheehy St
Forsyth St
Avon St
Fig St
Fig Lane Park
Ada St

Darling Harbour Passernger Terminal
Pyrmont Bay
To Pyrmont Bay
AIDC Tower
Hickson Rd
Western Distributor
Grosvenor St
Lang Park
Establishment Hotel
Lang St
Jamison St
Rydges
Westpac Plaza
Australia Square Tower
Wynyard
KPMG Tower
Westpac Place
Kent St
Clarence St
York St
Carrington St
Wynyard La
George St
Historical Vessel
Wharf 10
National Maritime Museum
King Street Wharf
Portside North/South Towers
Lime St
Shelley St
Erskine St
Wynyard St
Angel Pl
Martin Pl
Barrack St
The Western Sydney
Pyrmont Bay Wharf
Historical Vessels
Medina Grand Harbourside
Sydney Wildlife World
King St
Sussex St
Forum The Grace
Sydney Arcade
Pyrmont Bay
National Maritime Museum
Darling Harbour Wharf
Sydney Aquarium
Four Points by Sheraton
Mid City Centre
Sydney Central Plaza
Harbourside
Mercure Grand Apts
Pyrmont Bridge
Historical Vessels
Darling Park
Queen Victoria Bldg
City Centre
Murray St
Darling Dr
Ibis
Harbourside
Cockle Bay Wharf
Tower 1 IBM Centre
Capital Centre
Hilton Sydney
Water Taxi
Wheat Rd
Tunnel
Mullins St
Galeries Victoria
Cockle Bay
Novotel
Convention
Convention
Sydney Convention Centre
Aquamagic
Druitt La
Druitt St
City Group Tower
Sydney Town Hall
Town Hall
IMAX Theatre
Crowne Plaza
St Andrews Cathedral
Park House
Maestri Tower 2
Millennium Tower
Bathurst St
Sydney Exhibition Centre
Medina Grand
MBF Centre
HSBC
1000 ft
300 m
Exhibition Centre
Tumbalong Park
James St
Harbour St
Wilmot St
Central St
Century Bldg
Quay West
Four Seasons
Underwood
Dalley St
Bridge St
Bond St
CBD
Hosking
Pitt St
MLC Centre
Bank of America Centre
Skygarden
Imperial Arcade
Centrepoint
Market St
Piccadilly Tower
Sheraton on the Park
Galeries Victoria
Central Park
Park St
Leisure Park
Defence Plaza
Tunnel
Telstra House
Metro
Museum
Hyde Park Inn
228
228
233
D
E
F
D
E
F
1
2
3
4
4
4
76
40
40
30
10
22
12
38
26
17
13
88
29
40
20
14
7
11
14
13
34
87
37

N
A
B
C
230
1
2
3
4
GLEBE
ULTIMO
Glebe
Wentworth Park
Sports House
Greyhound Track
Fig Lane Park
Ultimo Primary School
City of Sydney Depot
Dr Foley Park
Glebe School
Broadway Shopping Centre
Unilodge
Macleay Museum
Womens Tennis Court
Baxters Lodge
Lake Northam
Aquatic Centre
Badham Bldg
Main Quardrangle
Maclaurin Hall
Fisher Library
Anderson Stuart Bldg
E David Bldg
Victoria Park
UTS
Bridge Rd
Taylor St
Bridge La
Railway St
Cardigan St
Darghan St
Darghan La
Bellvue St
Bellvue La
Wentworth Park Rd
Wattle St
Fig St
Jones St
Ada Pl
Harris St
Bulwara Rd
Quarry St
Broughton St
Darling St
Lyndhurst St
Darling La
St Johns Rd
William Henry St
Colbourne Ave
Brougham La
Brougham St
Gottenham La
Gottenham St
Talfourd St
Talfourd La
Denman La
Phillip St
Mitchell La
Wentworth St
Cowper St
Elger St
Bay St
Macarthur St
Mckee St
Wattle La
Norton St
Glebe St
Broughton La
Mitchell St
Campbell St
Glebe La
Queen St
Crown St
Bay La
Blackwattle La
Kelly St
Mountain La
Mountain St
Derwent La
Gerwent St
Campbell La
Glebe Point Rd
Cowper St
Franklyn St
Greek St
Kettle La
Small St
Westmoreland St
Francis St
St Barnabas St
Catherine St
Grose St
Great Western Highway
Arundel St
Knox St
University Pl
University Ave
City Rd
Myrtle La
Rose St
Shepherd La
Shepherd St
Moorgate La
Moorgate St
Paints La
Buckland St
Levey St
Myrtle St
Pine La
Pine St
Maze La
Fisher Rd
300 m
1000 ft
1
6
12
31
54
69

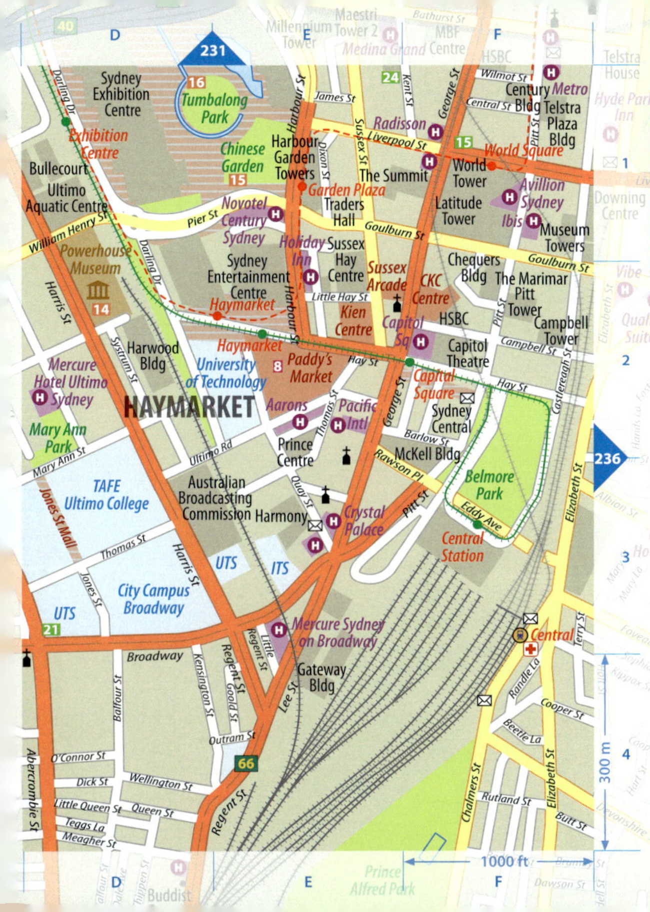
HAYMARKET
Sydney Exhibition Centre
Tumbalong Park
Chinese Garden
Harbour Garden Towers
Exhibition Centre
Bullecourt
Ultimo Aquatic Centre
Powerhouse Museum
Novotel Century Sydney
Sydney Entertainment Centre
Haymarket
Garden Plaza
Traders Hall
The Summit
Radisson
World Tower
Latitude Tower
World Square
Century Metro
Telstra Plaza Bldg
Avillion Sydney
Ibis
Museum Towers
Holiday Inn
Sussex Hay Centre
Sussex Arcade
CKC Centre
Chequers Bldg
The Marimar
Pitt Tower
Campbell Tower
Kien Centre
Capitol Sq
HSBC
Capitol Theatre
Harwood Bldg
University of Technology
Paddy's Market
Mercure Hotel Ultimo Sydney
Mary Ann Park
Aarons
Pacific Intl
Capital Square
Sydney Central
Prince Centre
McKell Bldg
Belmore Park
TAFE Ultimo College
Australian Broadcasting Commission
Harmony
Crystal Palace
Central Station
UTS
ITS
City Campus Broadway
Mercure Sydney on Broadway
Gateway Bldg
Central
Maestri Tower 2
Millennium Tower
Medina Grand
MBF Centre
HSBC
Telstra House
Museum
Hyde Park Inn
Downing Centre
Vibe
Quality Suites
Furama Hotel Central
Prince Alfred Park
Buddist
Darling Dr
William Henry St
Pier St
Harbour St
James St
Sussex St
Dixon St
Kent St
George St
Liverpool St
Goulburn St
Wilmot St
Central St
Pitt St
Little Hay St
Hay St
Campbell St
Castlereagh St
Harris St
Systrum St
Thomas St
Ultimo Rd
Barlow St
Rawson Pl
Eddy Ave
Quay St
Mary Ann St
Jones St Mall
Jones St
Elizabeth St
Broadway
Balfour St
Kensington St
Regent St
Goold St
Little Regent St
Lee St
Outram St
O'Connor St
Dick St
Wellington St
Little Queen St
Queen St
Teggs La
Meagher St
Abercrombie St
Chalmers St
Randle La
Cooper St
Beetle La
Rutland St
Butt St
Terry St
Albion St
Foveaux St
Belmore La
Devonshire St
300 m
1000 ft
D
E
F
1
2
3
4
231
236
40
24
15
16
14
8
21
66

N
A
B
C
1
2
3
4
229
236
Four Seasons
Justice & Police Museum
Sir Stamford at Circular Quay
Sydney Harbour Marriott
AMP Centre Tower
InterContinental
Conservatorium of Music
Dalley St
Bridge St
Establishment Hotel
Museum of Sydney
6
Young St
Loftus St
Pitt St
George St
Bent St
Bond St
Spring St
O'Connell St
Phillip La
Macquarie St
Tunnel
Royal Botanic Gardens
8
Macquarie Wall
The Wentworth
Radisson Plaza
19
Bligh St
Phillip St
Hunter St
17
Nursery
32
Royal Botanic Shop
State Library of NSW
Parliament House
Cahill Expressway
CBD
Castlereagh St
Elizabeth St
Hosking Pl
11
Hospital Rd
Martin Place
Martin Pl
The Western Sydney
MLC Centre
18
Sydney Hospital & Sydney Eye Hospital
The Domain
Art Gallery of NSW
5
Bank of America Centre
Skygarden
Imperial Arcade
9
King St
Old Supreme Court
Mint
7 Museum
Barracks Museum
Art Gallery Rd
St James Rd
Prince Albert St
City Centre
Centrepoint
Market St
St James
Archibald Fountain
St Mary's Cathedral
St Marys Rd
St Marys Cathedral College
4
Cathedral St
23
Piccadilly Tower
16
CapitalCentre
Hilton
Sheraton on the Park
Hyde Park
Galeries Victoria
Central Park
Park St
3
College St
86
Cook & Phillip Park
Yurong Pky
Broughton St
Turner La
Riley St
Kennedy St
Faucett La
Palmer St
Egan Pl
Bourke St
Sutton St
Robinson St
Leisure Inn Park
76
300 m
Defence Plaza
Tunnel
Australian Museum
45
William St
Telstra House
1000 ft
Metro
Museum
Anzac Memorial
Sydney Grammar School
The Avery Bldg
Stanley St
Crown St
Rosella La
Telstra Plaza Bldg
Century Bldg
Sydney Town Hall
Town Hall House
Queen Victoria Bldg
Mid City Centre
Pitt Street Mall
Sydney Arcade
Sydney Central Plaza
Wynyard St
Wynyard La
Carrington St
Barrack St
Bathurst St
MBF Centre
HSBC
Wilmot St
Mullins St

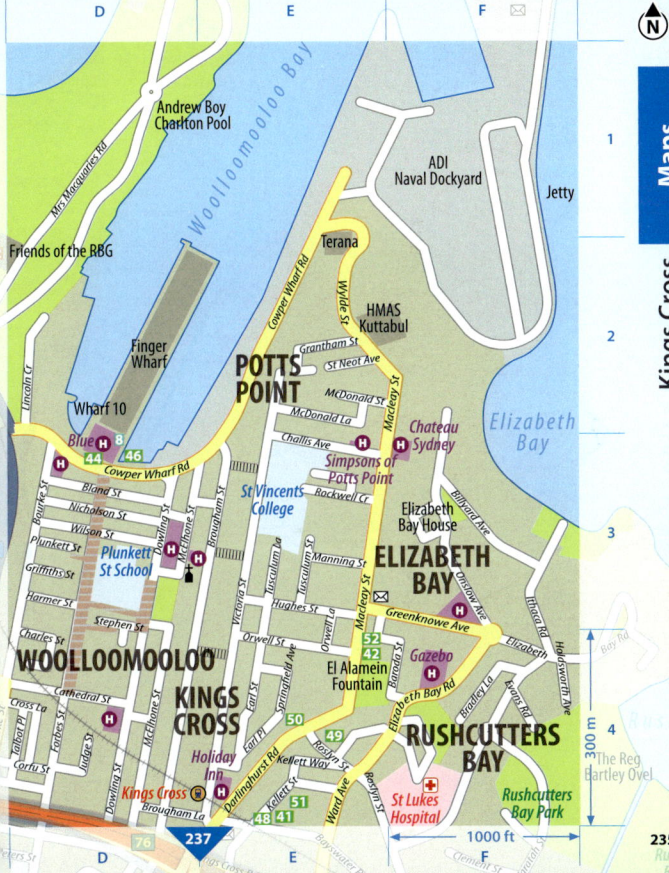

Kings Cross Maps

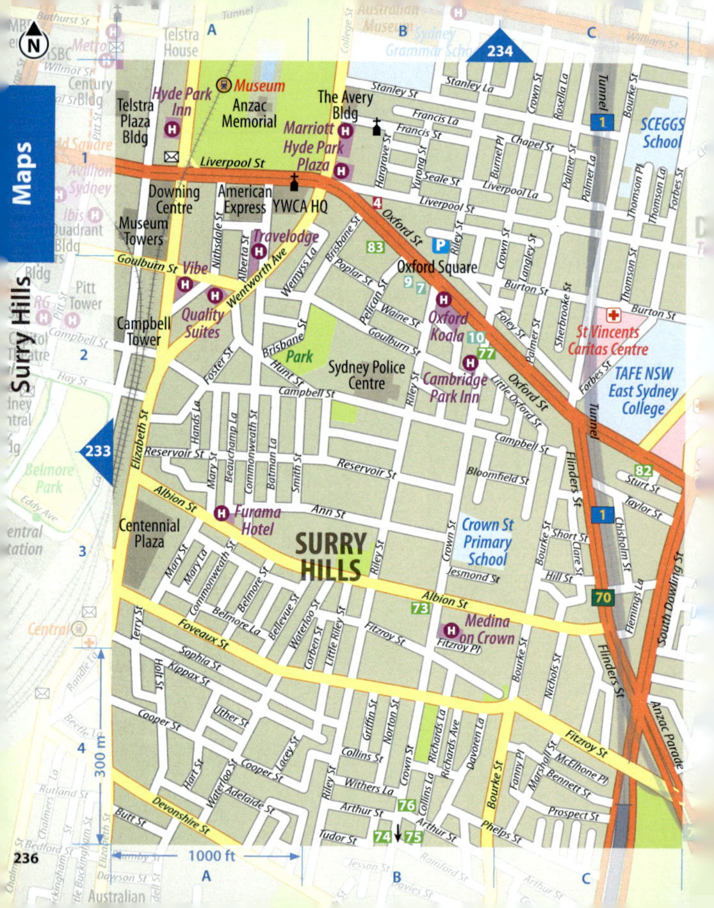
N
A
B
C
1
2
3
4
234
233
1000 ft
300 m
Telstra House
Australian Museum
Sydney Grammar School
Telstra Plaza Bldg
Hyde Park Inn
Museum
Anzac Memorial
The Avery Bldg
Marriott Hyde Park Plaza
Downing Centre
American Express
YWCA HQ
Museum Towers
Travelodge
Vibe
Quality Suites
Campbell Tower
Park
Sydney Police Centre
Oxford Square
Oxford Koala
Cambridge Park Inn
St Vincents Caritas Centre
TAFE NSW East Sydney College
SCEGGS School
Centennial Plaza
Furama Hotel
SURRY HILLS
Crown St Primary School
Medina on Crown
Century Bldg
Pitt Tower
Belmore Park
Central
Liverpool St
Goulburn St
Wentworth Ave
Oxford St
Elizabeth St
Reservoir St
Albion St
Foveaux St
Campbell St
Crown St
Riley St
Bourke St
Flinders St
Fitzroy St
Devonshire St
Cooper St
Stanley St
Francis St
Burton St
South Dowling St
Anzac Parade
Tunnel
83
9
7
10
77
82
70
73
76
74
75
4
1

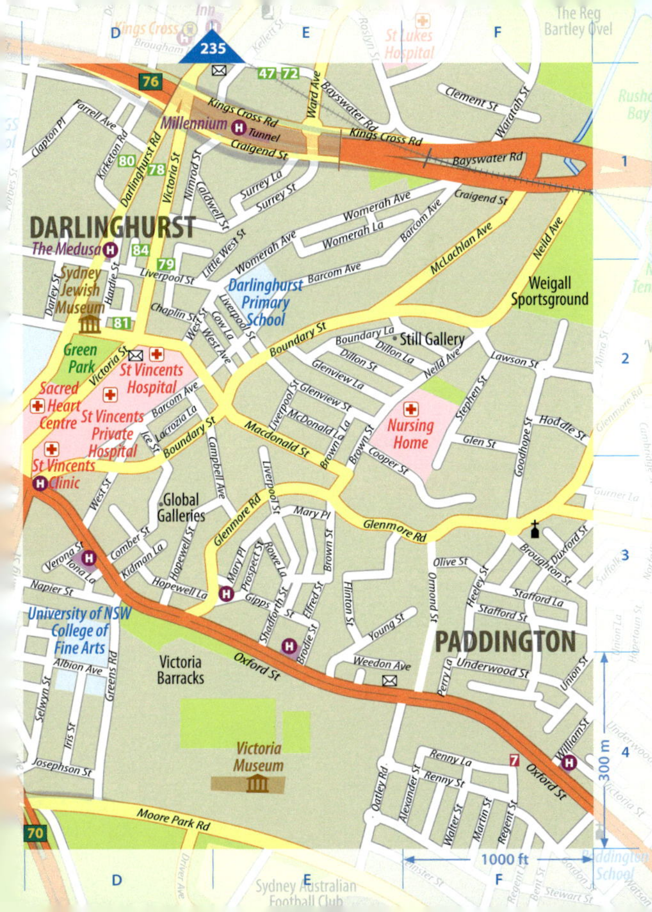
D
E
F
1
2
3
4
235
76
47
72
80
78
84
79
81
70
7
DARLINGHURST
PADDINGTON
Kings Cross
St Lukes Hospital
The Reg Bartley Oval
Millennium
Tunnel
Kings Cross Rd
Bayswater Rd
Craigend St
Ward Ave
Clement St
Waratah St
Farrell Ave
Clapton Pl
Kirketon Rd
Darlinghurst Rd
Victoria St
Nimrod St
Caldwell St
Surrey La
Surrey St
Womerah Ave
Womerah La
Barcom Ave
McLachlan Ave
Neild Ave
Little West St
The Medusa
Sydney Jewish Museum
Darley St
Hardie St
Liverpool St
Chaplin St
West St
Cow La
West Ave
Darlinghurst Primary School
Weigall Sportsground
Boundary St
Boundary La
Still Gallery
Dillon La
Dillon St
Glenview La
Glenview St
Lawson St
Stephen St
Green Park
Victoria St
St Vincents Hospital
Sacred Heart Centre
St Vincents Private Hospital
St Vincents Clinic
Barcom Ave
Lacrozia La
Ice St
McDonald La
Brown La
Brown St
Cooper St
Macdonald St
Nursing Home
Hoddle St
Glen St
Goodhope St
Campbell Ave
Global Galleries
Glenmore Rd
Mary Pl
Gurner La
Verona St
Iona La
Comber St
Kidman La
Hopewell St
Hopewell La
Napier St
Prospect St
Rowe La
Gipps St
Shadforth St
Elfred St
Flinton St
Olive St
Ormond St
Heeley St
Broughton St
Oxford St
Duxford St
Stafford La
Stafford St
University of NSW College of Fine Arts
Albion Ave
Greens Rd
Selwyn St
Iris St
Josephson St
Victoria Barracks
Victoria Museum
Brodie St
Young St
Weedon Ave
Perry La
Underwood St
Union St
William St
Renny La
Renny St
Oatley Rd
Alexander St
Walter St
Martin St
Regent St
Moore Park Rd
300 m
1000 ft
Sydney Australian Football Club
Paddington School
Driver Ave

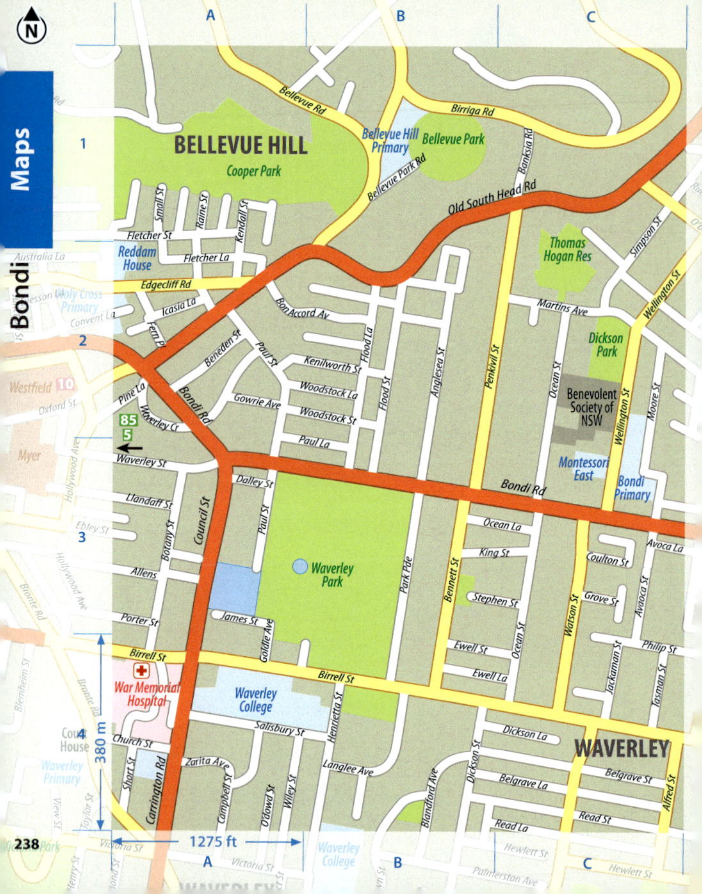
N
A
B
C
1
2
3
4
BELLEVUE HILL
Cooper Park
Bellevue Rd
Birriga Rd
Bellevue Hill Primary
Bellevue Park
Bellevue Park Rd
Banksia Rd
Old South Head Rd
Small St
Raine St
Kendall St
Fletcher St
Fletcher La
Reddam House
Australia La
Edgecliff Rd
Icasia La
Convent La
Holy Cross Primary
Fern Pl
Bon Accord Av
Beneden St
Paul St
Kenilworth St
Flood La
Flood St
Anglesea St
Penkivil St
Thomas Hogan Res
Simpson St
Wellington St
Martins Ave
Dickson Park
Ocean St
Benevolent Society of NSW
Moore St
Westfield
Oxford St
Pine La
Waverley Cr
Bondi Rd
Gowrie Ave
Woodstock La
Woodstock St
Paul La
85
5
Myer
Waverley St
Hollywood Ave
Dalley St
Montessori East
Bondi Primary
Llandaff St
Ebley St
Botany St
Council St
Ocean La
Avoca La
King St
Coulton St
Allens
Waverley Park
Park Pde
Bennett St
Stephen St
Grove St
Avaoca St
Bronte Rd
Porter St
James St
Goldie Ave
Watson St
Jackaman St
Philip St
Tasman St
Ewell St
Ewell La
Birrell St
War Memorial Hospital
Waverley College
Henrietta St
Salisbury St
Dickson La
WAVERLEY
Court House
Church St
Zarita Ave
Langlee Ave
Dickson St
Belgrave La
Belgrave St
Waverley Primary
Short St
Carrington Rd
Campbell St
Oldown St
Wiley St
Blandford Ave
Read La
Read St
Alfred St
380 m
1275 ft
Victoria St
Hewlett St
Palmerston Ave
View St
Taylor St
Blenheim St

D
E
F
N
1
2
3
4
Blair St
Beach Rd
Glasgow Ave
Warners Ave
Hastings PDE
Wairoa Special School
Simpson St
Wellington St
Curlewis St
Roscoe St
BONDI BEACH
Gould St
Ramsgate Ave
Wairoa Ave
Rudolf La
Maccabi Tennis Club
Hall St
Glenayr Ave
Beach Rd
Bondi Beach Primary
Warners Ave
O'brien St
Curlewis St
Swiss Grand
O'brien St
Roscoe St
Gould St
Park Gate Dr
Bondi Park
Barracluff Ave
Richard Ave
Cox Ave
Hall St
Chambers Ave
Consett Ave
Jaques Ave
Campbell Pde
Queen Elizabeth Dr
Francis St
BONDI
Lamrock Ave
Bondi Beach
Edward St
Ormond St
Skate Gate Park
Imperial Ave
Miller St
Castlefield St
Sir Thomas Mitchell Rd
Bondi Bay
Denham St
Denham La
Lucius St
Castlefield La
Cutler St
Edward St
Francis St
Campbell Pde
Notts Ave
Bondi Rd
Bondi Baths & Bondi Icebergs Club
Boonara La
Boonara Ave
Denham St
Glen St
Dudley St
Sandridge St
Andrews Ave
Hunters Park
Farrellys Av
Glen Ave
Wilga St
Rowland Ave
Illawong Ave
Tasman Sea
Tamarama St
Fletcher St
Wonderland Ave
Dell View St
Fletcher St
Dellview La
Carlisle St
Silva St
Alexander St
Kenneth St
Marks Park
Mackenzies Point
Tamarama Park
Cross St
Ashley St
Wolaroi Cr
Gaerloch Ave
TAMARAMA
Pacific Ave
Mackenzies Bay
Turner St
Darling St
Thompson St
380 m
1275 ft

A
B
C
1
2
3
4
Spring St
Mount St
Elizabeth Plaza
Walker St
Little Walker St
Arthur St
Warringah Freeway
Alfred St
Little Alfred St
Nicholas St
Neutral St
Dorris St
Bray St
Whaling Rd
The Avenue
Pile Pl
Anderson Park
Clark Rd
Spruson St
Ben Boyd Rd
Aubin St
Kurraba
Wycombe La
Manna Ave
Hayes St
Australian Customs
Neutral Bay
Neutral Bay Wharf
Pacific Highway
North Sydney
High St
Adderstone Ave
James Milson Nursery Home & Retirement Village
Former HMAS Platypus Site
Walker St
Walker La
Arthur St
Middlemiss St
Arthur La
Lavender St
Mcdougall St
Hipwood St
Bradly Ave
Milson Park
Kesterton Park
Stannards Pl
North Sydney Wharf
Clark Park
Harbour View Cr
Lavender Bay Wharf
Greenway Dr
Bradfield Highway
Winslow St
Winslow La
18ft Sailing Club
Ensemble Theatre
Willoughby St
Careening Cove
MILSONS POINT
Cliff St
Milsons Point
Crescent Pl
St Aloysius Junior Campus
Bligh St
KIRRIBILLI
Lavender Bay
Loreto Kirribilli
Fitzroy St
Elamang Av
Glen St
Fitzroy St
Bradfield Park
Robertson La
Jeffreys St
Carabella St
Parkes St
Royal Sydney Yacht Squadron
Luna Park
Dind St
Northcliff St
South St
Pitt St
Upper Pitt St
Mcburney La
Peel St
Broughton St
St Aloysius Senior Campus
Paul St
Sella
Holbrook Ave
Mcmahons Point Wharf
Milsons Point Wharf
North Sydney Olympic Pool
Bus Circle
Broughton Dr
Kirribilli St
Jeffrey St Wharf
MILSONS POINT
KIRRIBILLI
Carabella St
Waruda Ave
Beulah St
Plunkett St
Sydney Harbour Tunnel
Milsons Point
Waruda St
Kirribilli House
380 m
Sydney Harbour Bridge
Beulah St Wharf
Admiralty House
1275 ft
Kirribilli Point
20
21
5
69
70
71
91

A
B
C
1
2
3
4
NEWTOWN
MACDONALDTOWN
ERSKINEVILLE
Camperdown Memorial Rest Park
St Stephens Cemetery
St Andrews College
Newtown North Primary
University of Sydney
Hollis Park
Green Ban Park
Newtown High School of Performing Arts
Newtown Primary
Erskineville Primary
St Marys
Buddist Temple
Town Hall
Newtown
Macdonaldtown
Erskineville
Kuleto's Bar
Cooper's Arms Hotel
Carlisle Castle Hotel
Zanzibar
Banks Hotel
Town Hall Hotel
Imperial Hotel
Erskineville Hotel
Rose of Australia Hotel
New Tourist Hotel
Union Hotel
61
60
62
63
64
66
67
3
Carillon Ave
Salisbury Rd
King St
Missenden Rd
Wilson St
Enmore Rd
Erskineville Rd
Federation Rd
Lennox St
Albert St
Bridge Railway Pde
Swanson St
Copeland Ave
Burren St
Alice St
Macdonald St
Ashmore St
Railway
Camperdown Park
Harper House College
St Pauls College
Darlington Centre
South Sydney Rotary Park
Kurrajong Hotel
The Harry Noble Reserve
Erskineville Park
Lady Gowrie Child Centre
Mitchell Industrial Estate
Ashmore Industrial Estate
Camdenville
380 m
1275 ft
N
Explore

Manly

N
A
B
C
1
2
3
4
Sydney Rd
Parkview Rd
Griffiths Rd
Birkley Rd
Lawson Pl
Quinton Rd
Ocean La
Augusta Rd
Kangaroo Park
Pittwater Rd
Carlton St
Whistler St
Griffin St
George St
James St
Camera St
Raglan St
Ocean Rd
Augusta La
Kangaroo St
Smith St
Steinton St
North Steyne
Ivanhoe Park
Denison St
Gilbert St
Rowe St
Tower St
Belgrave St
The Crescent
Tower Hill Park
Eustace St
West Promenade St
Whistler St
Short St
North Steyne Beach
Imperial Hotel
Oceanworld Manly
Sydney Rd
Central Ave
Manly Pacific Sydney
West Esplanade
Belgrave St
Whistler St
New Brighton Hotel
Henrietta La
MANLY
Market Pl
The Corso
Ivanhoe Hotel
Hotel Steyne
Tasman Sea
Manly Wharf
Town Cinema
Darley Rd
Manly Beach
Wentworth St
To Circular Quay
School
Manly Cove
East Esplanade
Victoria Pde
South Steyne
Eversham Private Hotel
Manly Slsc
Manly Yacht Club
Sailing Club
Ashburner St
Bower St
Cabbage Tree Bay Aquatic Reserve
Cabbage Tree Bay
Cliff St
Cove Ave
Wood St
Osborne Rd
Reddall St
Darley Rd
Addison Rd
Fairy Bower
Addison Rd
Oyama Ave
Manly Waters Private Hospital
High St
Fairybower Rd
College St
Bower St
Smedleys Pt
380 m
Craig Ave
Stuart St
Wood St
Osborne Rd
Vivian St
Marshall St
Little Manly Cove
International College of Tourism & Hotel Management
1275 ft
Carey St
Gilroy House
St Pauls Catholic College
Darley Rd
Moran House
27
28
2
19
53
58
90
59
57
18
1
6
54

Legend

These maps include what we feel are the most interesting bits of Sydney. Bars, shops, areas to explore and activities and spas are marked with colour coded symbols (see below).

You may also have noticed the large pull-out map at the back of the book. This is intended to give you an overview of the city. The perforated edges mean you can detatch it from the main book, so you have even less to carry about with you. Or, if you and a travel companion have different plans for the day, you can take one each. So if one of you wants to shop, while the other wants to surf, there's no need for compromise.

48 Exploring   **48 Going Out**   **48 Shopping**   **48 Sports & Spas**

Legend

H *Hotel/Resort*	Sand/Beach	Highway
Heritage/Museum	Pedestrian Area	Major Road
Hospital	Built up Area/Building	Secondary Road
Park/Garden	Industrial Area	Other Road or Track
CityRail Station	Water	Tunnel
Shopping	Post Office	CityRail
Education	Church	CityRail Subway
2 Road No.	CBD Area Name	Light Rail
		Monorail
		Ferry Route
		Steps

Sydney Ferries

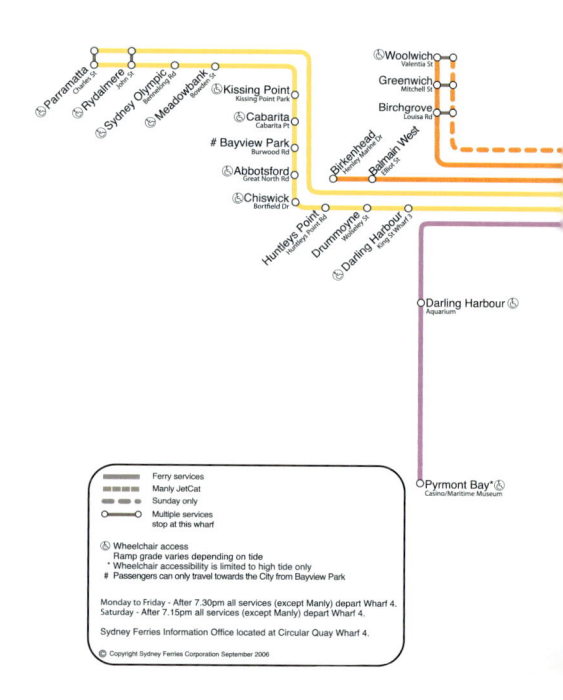

Maps

Ferries Map

- Parramatta — Charles St
- Rydalmere — John St
- Sydney Olympic — Bennelong Rd
- Meadowbank — Bowden St
- Kissing Point — Kissing Point Park
- Cabarita — Cabarita Pt
- \# Bayview Park — Burwood Rd
- Abbotsford — Great North Rd
- Chiswick — Bortfield Dr
- Huntleys Point — Huntleys Point Rd
- Drummoyne — Wolseley St
- Darling Harbour — King St Wharf 3
- Birkenhead — Huntley Point Rd
- Balman West — Elliot St
- Woolwich — Valentia St
- Greenwich — Mitchell St
- Birchgrove — Louisa Rd
- Darling Harbour — Aquarium
- Pyrmont Bay* — Casino/Maritime Museum

Legend:
- Ferry services
- Manly JetCat
- Sunday only
- Multiple services stop at this wharf
- ♿ Wheelchair access — Ramp grade varies depending on tide
- * Wheelchair accessibility is limited to high tide only
- \# Passengers can only travel towards the City from Bayview Park

Monday to Friday - After 7.30pm all services (except Manly) depart Wharf 4.
Saturday - After 7.15pm all services (except Manly) depart Wharf 4.

Sydney Ferries Information Office located at Circular Quay Wharf 4.

© Copyright Sydney Ferries Corporation September 2006

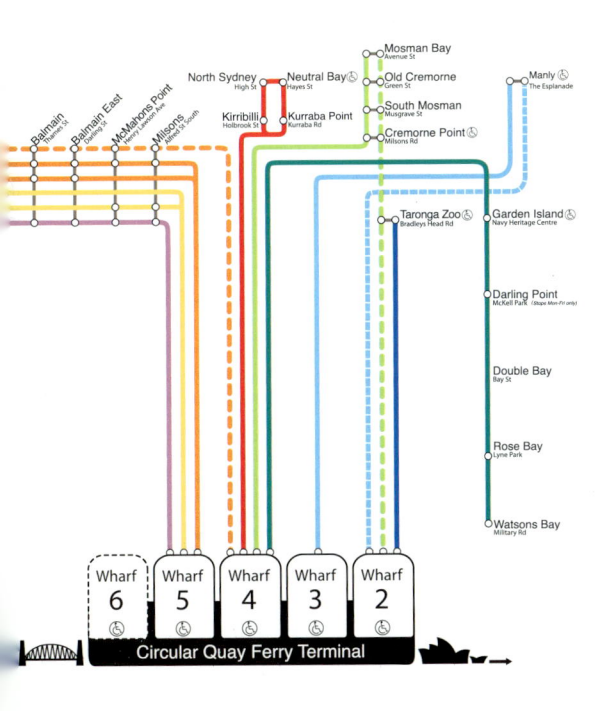

Maps

Sydney Ferries

Balmain
Thames St

Balmain East
Darling St

McMahons Point
Henry Lawson Ave

Milsons
Milsons South

North Sydney
High St

Neutral Bay
Hayes St

Mosman Bay
Avenue St

Old Cremorne
Green St

Manly
The Esplanade

Kirribilli
Holbrook St

Kurraba Point
Kurraba Rd

South Mosman
Musgrave St

Cremorne Point
Milsons Rd

Taronga Zoo
Bradleys Head Rd

Garden Island
Navy Heritage Centre

Darling Point
McKell Park (Stops Mon-Fri only)

Double Bay
Bay St

Rose Bay
Lyne Park

Watsons Bay
Military Rd

Wharf 6 | **Wharf 5** | **Wharf 4** | **Wharf 3** | **Wharf 2**

Circular Quay Ferry Terminal

Sydney **mini** Explorer   245

Index

#
360 Bar and Dining	163

A
Abbey on King	48
Aboriginal and Torres Strait Islander Commission	215
Aboriginal flag	217
Aboriginal Heritage Tour	105
Aborigines Welfare Board	215
Abyss Scuba Diving	111
Activities	110
Activity Tours	100
Advance Australia Fair	217
African Feeling	189
Airlines	19
Airport	18
Alfred Park Budget Hotel	49
Alhambra Café and Tapas Bar	185
Altamont (hotel)	47
Amora Hotel Jamison	49
Annual Events	30
ANZAC	214
Anzac Day	30
Aperitif	179
Aquablue	113
Aquarium	76
Arabella	189
Architecture Walks	106
Art Gallery of NSW	63, 202
Arun Thai	179
Ausail	113
Aussie Rules	118
Australia Day	30, 32
Australia Post	27
Aveda Concept Salon & Spa	122
Avis	38

B
Bali bombing	217
Bambini Trust Café	163
Bank Hotel	189
Bars	
...Bubble	171
...ECQ	172
...Iguana Bar & Restaurant	181
...The Blu Horizon Bar	171
...The Bourbon	179
...The Firehouse	193
...The Loft Bar	176
...The Victoria Room	199
Bathers' Pavilion	186
Beachwear	144
Belvoir Street Theatre	203
Best of Sydney	16
Bicycle	39
Big Hostel	48
Bills	195
Billy Kwong	195
Bilson's Restaurant	171
Birkenhead Point	138
Bligh	212
Blue	49
Blue Mountains	95
Blue Mountains Walkabout	105
Blue Sky Helicopters	104
Blu Horizon Bar	171
Boat Tours	102
Bodhi in the Park	163
Bondi & Around	56
Bondi	158
Bondi Beach	57
Bondi Beach Christmas Party	34
Bondi Explorer	38
Bondi Golf Course	112

Index

Bondi Icebergs Club	117	CBD		**D**	
Bondi Markets	136	...Exploring	62	Darling Harbour & Chinatown	
Bondi Social	159	...Going Out	162	...Exploring	74
Bondi to Bronte Cliff Walk	59	Cellar St	94	...Going Out	174
Bondi YHA	48	Central Coast & Newcastle	96	Darlinghurst	194
Bonza Bike Tours	101	Central Railway Hotel	49	David Jones	142
Books	29, 147	China Doll	180	Day of Mourning	216
Bounce Walking Tours	106	Chinatown	74, 174	Department Stores	142
Boutique Wine Tours	107	Chinese Garden	75	DFO	140
Bradfield Park	91	Chinese Laundry	164	DHL	27
Bridge Climb	68	Chinta Ria, Temple of Love	175	Didgeridoos	148
Bristol Arms Retro Hotel	164	Cinemas	201	Dive Centre Manly	111
Broadway Shopping Centre	138	Circular Quay & The Rocks		Diving	111
Bronte Beach	58	...Exploring	68	Dollar sign	42
Bubble Champagne		...Going Out	170	Domain, The	654
Cocktail Lounge	171	CityRail	40	Domain Theatre	203
Budget Accomodation	38	City Sightseeing	103	Dos & Don'ts	23
Bus	37	Climate	22	Drinking	156
Bus Tours	103	Clock Hotel	196		
BusTripper	38	Club77	180	**E**	
		Coaches	37	Easter	30
C		Columbian Hotel	196	EastSail	114
Cabaret & Strip Shows	200	Comedy	201	ECQ Bar	172
Cafes		Concerts	202	Electricity & Water	23
...Bathers' Pavilion	186	Consulates	21	Embassies	21
...Bills	195	Coogee Beach	59	Emergency Numbers	23
...Gertrude & Alice	159	Cook, Captain James	210	Enmore Theatre	202
...Harry's Café de Wheels	180	Council for Aboriginal		Entertainment	200
...Macro Wholefoods Café	160	Reconciliation	217	Essentials	2
...MCA Café	173	CountryLink	40	Est	165
...Yellow Bistro	182	Courier Companies	27	Establishment	49
Café Mint	195	Crest Hotel	49	Europcar	38
Café Sydney	164	Cricket	119	Exchange Centres	24
Captain Cook Cruises	102	Crime & Safety	22		
Car	38	Cronulla riots	217	**F**	
Car Rental Agencies	38	Culture	206	Federal Express	27
Casapueblo	196	Customs	21	Federation	214
Casinos	200	Cycling	39	Ferry	36

Index

FerryTen tickets	36	Going Out	150	Hugo's Bar Pizza	181
First Fleet	210	Gold rush	216	Hunter Valley	94
Flickerfest	32	Golf	112	Hunter Valley Wine and	
Food & Drink	209	Govinda's Restaurant		Dine Carriages	107
Fort Denison	80	and Cinema	197	Hyde Park	62
Four Points Sheraton	49	Grace Hotel	44		
Four Seasons	49	Grand Taverna	165	**I**	
Freedom Rides	217	Green Gourmet	190	Icebergs Dining Room and Bar	159
From The Airport	18	Green Palace	190	Ice Cube Seafood Grill Bar	176
Front Restaurant and Bar	175	Green Park Hotel	197	Iguana Bar and Restaurant	181
		Greyhound	37	Illawarra	97
G		GST	131	Industrie – South of France	166
G'day	4	Guillaume at Bennelong	172	InterContinental	49
Gallipoli	214			Internet	26
Garfish	193	**H**		Italian Forum	141
Garrison Church	71	Hall Street, Bondi	132		
Gavala Aboriginal Art &		Harbour, The	80	**J**	
Cultural Centre		Harbour Breeze	49	Jellyfish	185
Gay & Lesbian	155	Harbour Bridge	68	Jobonga Massage &	
Gay and Lesbian Mardi Gras	33	harbourkitchen&bar	172	Natural Therapy	126
Gay & Lesbian Venues		Harbour National Park	81	Jolly Swagman	48
...Bank Hotel	189	Haroo	193		
...Club 77	180	Harry's Café de Wheels	180	**K**	
...Slide	198	Helicopter & Plane Tours	104	Kafenes	191
...The Columbian Hotel	196	Hellenic Club	166	Ka Huna Centre	126
George Hotel	49	Hermitage Walking Track	81	Kam Fook	160
Gertrude & Alice	159	Hertz	38	Kangaroo Valley	97
Getabout 4WD		Hilton	44	Kayaking	101, 113
Adventure Tours	100	History	210	Kings Cross & Woolloomooloo	
Getting Around	36	Home	175	...Going Out	178
glass brasserie	165	Homebake Festival	34	King Street	133
Glebe Healing Centre	125	Horse Racing	121	Kirketon	49
Glebe Markets	136	Hostels	48	Kirketon Dining Room & Bar	197
Glebe Point Road	132	Hotel59	47		
Glebe YHA	48	Hotspots (Shopping)	132	**L**	
Glenferrie Lodge	49	Howard, John	215	Labour Day	30
Globe Backpackers	48	Hughenden, The	44	Ladylux	181

Index

Language	208	Massage By The Sea at Wylie's Baths	126	...Tank	168
Let's Go Surfing	116			...Tonic Lounge	182
Light Rail	41	Maze Backpackers	49	North Fort	84
Lingerie	148	MCA Café	173	North Sydney	
Local Knowledge	22	McIvers Baths	117	...Exploring	90
Loft Bar	176	Medusa, The	45	...Going Out	192
Lord Nelson Brewery Hotel	45	Metro Theatre	202	North Sydney Olympic Pool	117
Lost & Found	23	Miilk Studio	124	Norton Street	133
Lunar Park	90	Miltons	167	Novotel	49
		Mint, The	65	Nu's	193
M		Money	24		
Macarthur	212	Monorail	41	**O**	
Macquarie, Lachlan	213	Moore Park Golf Course	112	Observatory	69
Macro Wholefoods Café	160	Moulin Rouge	182	Observatory Hotel, The	45
Magistic Cruises	102	Multicultural Sydney	218	Observatory Hotel Day Spa	124
Malay Chinese Takeaway	166	Murrays	37	Ocean Room	173
Malls	138	Museum of Contemporary Art	70	Oceanworld	86, 111
Manly		Museum of Sydney	64	Oh! Calcutta!	198
...Exploring	84	Myall Creek massacre	216	Opera House	69
...Going Out	184	Myer	142	Out of Africa	187
Manly Art Gallery & Museum	84			Oxford Street	134
Manly Beach	85	**N**			
Manly Ferry	103	National Maritime Museum	75	**P**	
Manly Guesthouse	48	Newcastle	96	Paddington Markets	137
Manly International Jazz Festival	34	New South Wales Corps	212	Paddy's Market	137
		Newspapers & Magazines	28	Park Hyatt	46
Manly Phoenix	185	Newton's Cucina	191	Parramatta Visitor Centre	21
Manly Quarantine Station	86	Newtown	188	Pemulwuy	216
Manly Scenic Walk	85	New Year's Eve	35	People With Disabilities	20
Manly Surf School	116	Nightclubs		Peter's of Kensington	143
Manly Visitor Centre	21	...Bristol Arms Retro Hotel	164	Phillip, Captain Arthur	212
Manly Wharf Hotel	187	...Chinese Laundry	164	Pitt Street Mall	139
Mardi Gras	33	...Home	175	Places to Stay	42
Markets	136	...Ladylux	181	Plane Tours	104
Marriott	49	...Moulin Rouge	182	Police	24
Massage	125	...Purple Sneakers	167	Post	27
		...Ruby Rabbit	198	Powerhouse Museum	75

Index

Premier	37	
Prime Restaurant	167	
Pubs		
...Green Park Hotel	197	
...The Clock Hotel	196	
...The Slip Inn	168	
Public Holidays	30	
Purple Sneakers	167	
Pylon Lookout	68	

Q

Quarantine Station	86
Quayside Charters	114
Queen Victoria Building	139

R

Radio	28
Radisson Plaza	46
Railway Square YHA	48
Raw Bar	160
Religion	209
Roads and Traffic Authority	39
Royal Botanic Gardens & Domain	65
Royal Easter Show	33
Ruby Rabbit	198
Rugby League	119
Rugby League Grand Final	34
Rugby League State of Origin	33
Rugby Union	120
Rum Corps	212
Rum Rebellion	216
Russell Hotel	49

S

S.H. Ervin	70
Sail Australia	114
Sailing	113
SEC	202
Semi-precious Stones	149
Shangri-La	49
Sharks	25
Shark Island	81
Sheraton on the Park	49
Shopping	128
Shopping Malls	138
Simply Sailing	114
Simpsons of Potts Point	46
Sinclairs	48
Sir Stamford	49
Skywalk	100
Slide	198
Snorkel Inn	112
Soccer	121
Sofitel Wentworth	49
Soul Day Spa	124
Southern Highlands	98
Souvenirs	149
Spa Chakra	125
Spas & Massage Centres	122
Spectator Sports	118
Spiders, Sharks & Stingers	25
Sports & Spas	110
State of Origin	33, 120
Steki Taverna	191
St Mary's Cathedral	63
Stolen Generation	215
Strine	208
Sullivans Hotel	49
Sumac	176
Surfing	116
Surry Hills & Darlinghurst	194
Susannah Place Museum	71
Swimming Baths	117
Swissotel Sydney	49
Sydney Aquarium	76
Sydney Art Theatre	203
Sydney By Seaplane	104
Sydney Central YHA	48
Sydney Explorer	38, 104
Sydney Festival	32
Sydney Harbour Bridge	68
Sydney Harbour Kayak	113
Sydney Harbour National Park	21, 81
Sydney Helitours	105
Sydney Observatory	69
Sydney Opera House	69, 202
Sydney Theatre Co.	203
Sydney to Hobart Yacht Race	35
Sydney Tower	64
Sydney Visitor Centre	21
Sydney Wildlife World	76

T

Tamarama Beach	59
Tank	168
Taronga Zoo	91
Taxi	39
Taxi Companies	40
Telephone	26
Television	28
Tent Embassy	217
Theatre	203
Theatre Royal	203
The Australian	49
The Basement	202
The Bourbon	179
The Firehouse	193
The Harbour	80
The Last Resort	123

The Rocks	
...Exploring	68
...Going Out	170
The Rocks Walking Tours	107
The Slip Inn	168
Thrifty	38
Time	27
Timeline	216
Tipping	27, 154
Toilets	27
Tonic Lounge	182
Tourist Information	21
Tours	100
Train	40
Tri-Nations Rugby	33
Tumbalong Park	76
Twilight at Taronga Series	32

U

UPS	27

V

Victoria Room	199
Vintage Clothing	146
Visas	20
Visiting Sydney	18
Visitor Information	21

W

Wake Up!	48
Walking Tours	105
Water Taxi	36
Waves Surf School	116
Websites	29
Westfield Bondi Junction	140
Westin, The	47
Where To Go For...	144

Whitlam, Gough	215
Wildlife World	76
Will & Toby's	186
Wine Tours	107
Wollongong & Illawarra	97
Woolloomooloo	178
Wylie's Baths	117

Y

Yellow Bistro & Food Store	182
Yellow Star	155
Yoshii	173

Z

Zaaffran	177

Explorer Products

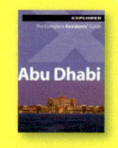

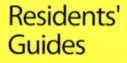

Residents' Guides

All you need to know about living, working and enjoying life in these exciting destinations

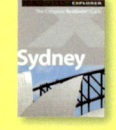

- Abu Dhabi
- Amsterdam *
- Bahrain
- Barcelona *
- Dubai
- Dublin *
- Geneva *
- Hong Kong
- Kuwait
- London
- New York
- New Zealand
- Oman
- Paris *
- Qatar
- Shanghai
- Singapore
- Sydney

* Covers not final. Titles available Winter 2007.

Mini Guides

Perfect pocket-sized visitors' guides

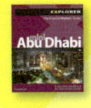

Abu Dhabi
Amsterdam
Bahrain *
Barcelona *
Dubai
Dublin
Hong Kong *
London
New York
New Zealand *
Oman
Paris *
Shanghai *
Singapore *
Sydney

* Covers not final. Titles available Winter 2007.

Activity Guides

Drive, trek, dive and swim... life will never be boring again

Oman off-road
Oman trekking
UAE underwater

Mini Maps
Fit the city in your pocket

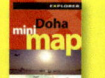

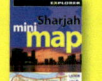

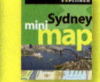

Abu Dhabi · Amsterdam · Bahrain
Barcelona · Doha · Dubai · Dublin · Hong Kong
Kuwait · London · Muscat · New York · Paris
Shanghai · Sharjah · Singapore · Sydney · UAE

✳ Covers not final. Titles available Winter 2007.

Maps
Wherever you are, never get lost again

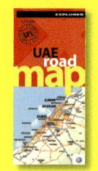

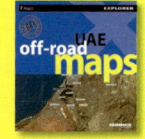

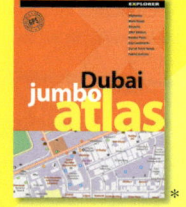

UAE road map · UAE off-road maps · Dubai jumbo atlas

✳ Cover not final.

Photography Books
Beautiful cities caught through the lens.

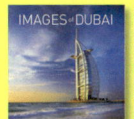

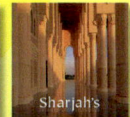

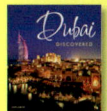

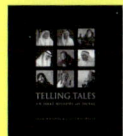

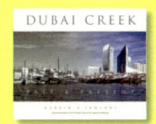

Lifestyle Products & Calendars
The perfect accessories for a buzzing lifestyle

Explorer Team

Publisher
Alistair MacKenzie

Editorial
Managing Editor Claire England
Lead Editors David Quinn, Jane Roberts, Matt Farquharson, Sean Kearns, Tim Binks, Tom Jordan
Deputy Editors Helen Spearman, Jake Marsico, Katie Drynan, Rebecca Wicks, Richard Greig, Tracy Fitzgerald
Editorial Assistants Grace Carnay, Ingrid Cupido, Mimi Stankova

Design
Creative Director Pete Maloney
Art Director Ieyad Charaf
Senior Designers Alex Jeffries, Iain Young
Layout Manager Jayde Fernandes
Designers Hashim Moideen, Rafi VP, Shefeeq Marakkatepurath, Sunita Lakhiani
Cartography Manager Zainudheen Madathil
Cartographer Noushad Madathil
Design Admin Manager Shyrell Tamayo
Production Coordinator Maricar Ong

IT
IT Administrator Ajay Krishnan R.
Senior Software Engineer Bahrudeen Abdul
Software Engineer Roshni Ahuja

Photography
Photography Manager Pamela Grist
Photographer Victor Romero
Image Editor Henry Hilos

Sales and Marketing
Area Sales Manager Stephen Jones
Marketing Manager Kate Fox
Retail Sales Manager Ivan Rodrigues
Retail Sales Coordinator Kiran Melwani
Corporate Sales Executive Ben Merrett
Digital Content Manager Derrick Pereira
Distribution Supervisor Matthew Samuel
Distribution Executives Ahmed Mainodin, Firos Khan, Mannie Lugtu
Warehouse Assistant Mohammed Kunjaymo
Drivers Mohammed Sameer, Shabsir Madathil

Finance and Administration
Administration Manager Andrea Fust
Financial Manager Michael Samuel
Accounts Assistant Cherry Enriquez
Administrators Enrico Maullon, Lennie Maugaliuo
Driver Rafi Jamal